LOVE
WILL
LIVE

A JOURNEY FROM BROKENNESS
TO RESTORATION

For Uta and Rachel

JENA KEENAN

WESTBOW
PRESS®

A DIVISION OF THOMAS NELSON
& ZONDERVAN

WestBow Press books may be ordered through booksellers or by contacting:

WestBow Press
A Division of Thomas Nelson & Zondervan
1663 Liberty Drive
Bloomington, IN 47403
www.westbowpress.com
844-714-3454

Because of the dynamic nature of the Internet, any web addresses or links contained in this book may have changed since publication and may no longer be valid. The views expressed in this work are solely those of the author and do not necessarily reflect the views of the publisher, and the publisher hereby disclaims any responsibility for them.

Any people depicted in stock imagery provided by Getty Images are models, and such images are being used for illustrative purposes only. Certain stock imagery © Getty Images.

Unless otherwise indicated, scripture quotations are taken from the Holy Bible, New Living Translation, copyright © 1996, 2004, 2007 by Tyndale House Foundation. Used by permission of Tyndale House Publishers, Inc., Carol Stream, Illinois 60188. All rights reserved.

Scripture quotations marked ESV are from the ESV Bible® (The Holy Bible, English Standard Version®), copyright © 2001 by Crossway Bibles, a publishing ministry of Good News Publishers. Used by permission. All rights reserved.

Scripture quotations marked NKJV are taken from the New King James Version. Copyright © 1982 by Thomas Nelson, Inc. Used by permission. All rights reserved.

ISBN: 979-8-3850-0052-4 (sc)
ISBN: 979-8-3850-0058-6 (e)

Library of Congress Control Number: 2023913701

Print information available on the last page.

WestBow Press rev. date: 08/01/2023

LOVE WILL LIVE

Introduction

Over the course of the years that I found myself writing this story, I never imagined some of the things that would play out in my life. I imagined my life to look very different from what it ended up looking like, and I had to let go of some expectations. I also never expected some of the connections to come about the way they did; I never expected any of it. I am continually blown away at how God works.

My only hope is that this story points to Jesus. I haven't painted myself in a glamourous light. This is raw and authentic and frankly, scares me to no end to have my story out there. But it's a story worth sharing because it's an incredible story about how Jesus can take something so broken and turn it into something so beautiful. He can take what I saw as completely unfixable and turn it into something so much better. It is undeniably Him.

I've had friends joke that I should write a book about how I was able to finish my book. I used to crave the feeling that I was in control of my life, but when my life, as I knew it fell apart, God literally held me up, sending the exact people that I needed to inspire me, support me, love me, encourage me. Those people showed up at the exact time I needed them in my life. To the day, to the hour. I cannot make this up; it's been so obvious who truly has control of my life.

To watch what I thought would be the worst things I could imagine happen, and then to see God take beauty from it all was incredible. So many things had to happen in the exact timing to work out the way it did. It wasn't always pretty, and it didn't feel nice for a long time, but once the connecting pieces fell together, it was truly something beautiful; something that was undeniably good. In fact, it was something better than I could ever imagine.

I was constantly being reminded that all things work together for the good. As I type this, "For the Good" by Riley Clemmons comes on. I've never heard this song before, but of course it was the song that comes on. God isn't always as blatantly obvious, but He has definitely been making Himself known. As I typed the last words in this book, I hit enter, sat back and took a huge breath- a sigh of relief, a final breath, a weight lifted off my shoulders, and "All In" by Matthew West came on; the last line he sings is "Welcome home, my child, well done". Flip to the last page, if you're into spoilers and you need a smile. Things like this have happened, time and time again.

It's all in God's hands, and it's so far beyond what I could even imagine as good. He truly takes what the world sees as impossible to prove what is truly possible. And while it's been painful and years of tears, it is completely worth it to see just how beautiful life is. It is not because of what I've done, but only because of what Jesus does. He has shown me incredible love and forgiveness. I am absolutely in awe of how He works, how He speaks, how He loves me. And you.

I didn't go on this journey alone. I've had amazing people show up in my life at the moments I needed them most. For the most part, they didn't even know what was truly going on. They showed up without me having to ask them because I had asked God. I had prayed for miracles and for support and for direction. Then specific people, the ones that God knew I needed, showed up. There were people that showed up in the most bizarre circumstances. Broken backs, hospital trips, every day appointments, places I shouldn't have been but found myself there anyways. No matter what the circumstance was, God would connect me to the person or people I needed.

There were reminders literally on billboards and Northern lights in the sky.

A quick and non-comprehensive list of those involved include: My family, friends, acquaintances, and even strangers along the way. Everyone has an impact on others, big or small, whether you know it or not. But you know who you are. You know your part.

I have always had the sense that God was beside me, no matter what, even when things didn't look like they were going well. It was especially during those times that He made Himself so obvious. There have been countless moments in my life where I couldn't pull myself out of bed, let alone survive what was being placed in my path. But every morning, I woke up and somehow made it through another day. It wasn't because I was strong and tough. Because we all know I'm not! But He has always carried me in my weakness, and that's exactly how strong He is, and stronger. He can carry so much more than I could ever carry. And that's why I need Him. I would not be here if it wasn't for His constant love towards me, His little kiddo who can't get anything right, it seems. He is so patient and kind. He's got this. I don't.

xo Jena

Coffee Shop

"Love will live."

Those were the words spoken to me by an older man, just as I walked into a local coffee shop to meet with a close friend. Why would those words be spoken to me, with nothing else said; no context, and no precursor; and especially at that moment in my life?

It left me feeling stunned. I asked my friend if she had just heard what that older man had just said. She said 'yes'. I just said 'weird', and we carried on our coffee date. But those words echoed in my soul, from the moment the mysterious older man spoke them, and have never left me since.

As we met and spent the next three hours with my friend, sitting in the corner of that small coffee shop, I explained to her how I had just opened a big can of worms.

The whole reason for being in the coffee shop that day makes me incredibly sad. The previous day, I had made a phone call that I had been thinking about making for a few months. That phone call was the can of worms.

About six and a half years prior, I had been sexually assaulted. Wow. There it is, in print. There is no hiding from that, whether it's in print or not. The news and social media had been covering circumstances similar to mine quite extensively over the months. A few very high profile sexual assault cases were coming to light, after years of silence from the victims.

As much as I wanted to forget the whole thing had ever happened, bitterness and resentment can destroy you. The pain would well up in a debilitating flurry of anxiety and depression, at any unexpected moment. Any healing was hindered with self-medicating in my feeble attempts to forget and bury the pain.

One sleepless night after watching a special on the victims of these horrible crimes, I knew it was finally time to do something about my own personal nightmare; my own, private inferno.

The problem with this timing was, now, it was six and a half years later. As I did the math that night, after watching the faces of numerous victims of sexual assault being interviewed, I realized it was time to face my own situation.

2008 felt suddenly very close again. The timing of making the call was feeling critical. I'm certainly no mathematician, but at that time, it was December of 2014. The incident had taken place in 2008. Having been in the insurance industry for a short time, I knew that businesses are required to keep their paperwork for seven years, and with some basic math, 2015 would be the seventh year.

Being December meant it was only weeks away now from the New Year, technically the seventh year, since the incident had happened. I knew those documents could potentially be destroyed, depending on the year end dates.

I nervously made the hesitant call to the HR department, explaining what had happened six years before. I vividly remember shaking as I spoke, requesting the only proof in the world that this had ever occurred.

The security department called me back right away gave me the file number of the altercation that happened in the days after the assault. I thought that was very helpful. A few hours later, I got another call from HR and suddenly, I needed a lawyer to write a formal request for the documents.

That day in the coffee shop, the day after requesting the files documenting the circumstances surrounding the assault, I needed to talk to my friend about the steps I was taking in finding out more information about the assault, while also discussing the probability of the information I had requested leading to nothing.

I had talked with a lawyer the day that I made the original phone call, who explained the statute of limitations about reporting a crime. In Canada, historical sexual assault does not apply to the statute of limitations, you can report a sexual assault any time, no matter what the timeframe.

That was a step in the right direction for me. I talked to the victim services through the RCMP that night, as well. She listened to my whole story and explained the process that would be involved should I decide to go to the RCMP. The next morning, before meeting my friend at the coffee shop, I got the lawyer to write the letter, and waited.

~

In 2008, I lived in beautiful Lake Louise. I worked at the Chateau Lake Louise, a picturesque and truly stunning resort destination for travelers. Even though Canada is the second largest country in the world, this tiny, gorgeous village seems to stand out amongst the rest.

As a Canadian traveling abroad, people assumed you were from either Toronto, Vancouver or Lake Louise. It was quite an idealistic place to live, I won't lie. It also offered a great outdoor lifestyle, which I took full advantage of, but it also had a dark side, to which I was quite vulnerable.

For those who actually live in Lake Louise, it is quite apparent that a year is about the maximum you can live there, unless you have the ability or desire to party for ten years straight.

Staff accommodation was similar to college dorm rooms, with that in mind, you can also imagine all that encompasses a college lifestyle, masked by some majestic mountain beauty and a healthy, outdoor lifestyle.

Party, sleep, hike, snowboard, work. Repeat. That's just what people did. And it was the norm; socially acceptable. Of course, we were all fresh out of college, and up for anything.

With all that partying, it's amazing that it took as long as it did for the assault to happen. I had lived there for two whole months. One night, after a day of festivities for my good friend's birthday, I hit that invisible drunken wall, and knew I needed to go home.

I walked home alone from the staff pub, where a guy intersected me on my stumble home. I had briefly spoken to him once before at the store I was working at, so he wasn't an unfamiliar face, and I had been nice to him. He said he would make sure I made it home safely, and I thought that was nice of him to be concerned for my safety.

He walked me back to my apartment; all I remember was crawling into bed, alone, with my world spinning, and then nothing. In the morning, I was horrifically woken up to this guy doing what he did to me. I lay there, terrified at the reality of this moment, yet pretending to still be asleep. I was absolutely trying to shut out at least the sight of what was happening to me, desperately trying to believe this wasn't happening. This was just a bad dream.

I continued to lay there silently, trying not to get sick. Thoughts were chaotically running through my head; ruthlessly blaming myself for being in a situation like this.

What were you thinking, Jena?? How could you let this situation happen? You deserved this. But God, please make it stop. Please protect me.

He finally left after this; perhaps thinking I had been asleep this whole time. When I finally opened my eyes, I couldn't see through my tears. I showered, trying to wash away the shame of what happened and tears continued to flow.

I lost a part of me that day. It was a part of me that could trust others, and a part of me that could trust myself. I felt so naïve and used and damaged. There is so much guilt and shame associated with a sexual assault. I couldn't handle it.

Between the shock and disgust at the reality of what had just happened, I kept to myself for a while. A few days later, I finally told a friend about what had gone on. Apparently, this wasn't the first story involving this guy. He knew this, and told his friend.

Although I was hoping for secrecy, these two guys confronted him over his actions. An altercation ensued, which subsequently got security involved. These two guys now had their jobs on the line because of the altercation over what had happened to me. I couldn't believe that. They were going to lose their jobs for defending me. What happened to me was already an injustice I could barely deal with emotionally.

I got called into HR a few days after this, and was asked to confirm if this was true. I told them everything. This is why I knew they had the incident on file. I was told that because he was a contractor, and not actually an employee at the

Chateau, there was nothing they could do. The renovations were completed a few days previously, and he was no longer there, so the problem was solved. And I just accepted that.

In harsh reality, I don't know who he is, or if he has done something like this again. It's likely, as I wasn't the first person he had done this to. Maybe he is dead now or in jail. Maybe he has a family. Maybe it's best that I never know.

I wish I had gotten better advice at that point, on how to deal with what had happened. I received no direction to report it to the police, and offered no support in the assault that had just occurred.

I spent the following years of my life trying to forget everything. I hardly remember much of my life in those years, but I remember desperately trying to mask my pain with alcohol, sex, drugs; which, in reality, sent my life spinning into a complete disaster.

This is where the punishment for the crime lands on the wrong individual. The one who is victimized by the crime is the one punished, again and again, serving an unjust life sentence, with no chance for parole.

My peace has been stripped away, and I have forgotten what prosperity is. I cry out, "My splendor is gone! Everything I had hoped for from the Lord is lost! The thought of my suffering and homelessness is bitter beyond words. I will never forget this awful time, as I grieve over my loss. Yet I dare to hope when I remember this: The faithful love of the Lord never ends! His mercies never cease. Great is his faithfulness; His mercies begin

**afresh each morning. I said to myself, "The Lord is
my inheritance; therefore I will hope in Him."**
(Lamentations 3:17-23)

As much as I did not want that day to affect the outcome of my life, it did. It inevitably changed me.

Jennifer Lawrence said it best.

*"It's my body, and it should be my choice, and the fact
that it is not my choice is absolutely disgusting. I can't
believe that we even live in that kind of world."*

I struggled with the guilt of it happening. I struggled with the broken trust I had in everyone. I struggled feeling dirty and used. I lost self-esteem and self-worth. I struggled to cope with life in a healthy way, and I found myself in a serious internal struggle to survive in my day to day life.

But you can push on through life. In some circumstances, God-willing, you can even thrive.

**Remember, O Lord, your compassion and unfailing
love, which you have shown from long ages past.
Do not remember the rebellious sins of my youth.
Remember me in the light of your unfailing love,
for you are merciful, O Lord. The Lord is good and
does what is right; he shows the proper path
for those who go astray.**
(Psalm 25:6-8)

It took me a lot of years, a lot of tears, a lot of therapy and a lot of forgiveness to look at it in a different light. No one immediately sees the bright side of something terrible. Most of all, it takes something bigger than yourself to help you hold on.

Yet More Brokenness

I won't say my issues started in Lake Louise. My mother always said something like 'your issues will follow you wherever you go, no matter where you run to.' Well, I always tried to run. And my mother turned out to be right.

From the surface, my life was pretty great. I lived in a nice house, in a safe, small community, with my loving family. We went to church every Sunday, and I did excellent in school, a small, private Christian school. I was involved in sports, like soccer, archery, track and field; you name it. My options in life were never limited.

I had really good friends, and we had so many great adventures. Like the time we fell through the ice when we decided we wanted to go rafting on the unthawed river, and having to trek back to the car, through the snow, soaking wet.

Or hide and go seek days amongst the hay bales and in the chicken barns, riding bikes through two feet of snow, and driving down country back roads in one of our parent's van, surfing on an old ironing board tied behind. Good, old fashioned fun- the stuff country songs are made of, but with punk blaring.

I wish that all the fun times were enough to keep me truly happy, but when I was not keeping busy, I was a sad little girl. I felt troubled, like the weight of the world was on my shoulders. I worried about the neighbourhood kids liking me, I worried about school; mostly I worried about being the perfect kid. Anything I could worry about, I tried my best to be the best, most perfect worrier.

Yet, I still clung to God. I knew it as a child. I didn't see it life as other's maybe did. I knew there was something more to life, something incredibly special. I was full of hope and peace and surrounded by love. However, as a child, I did not expect life to be as dark as it was.

When I was a child, I spoke and thought and reasoned like a child. But when I grew up, I put away childish things. Now we see things imperfectly, like puzzling reflections in a mirror, but then we will see everything with perfect clarity. All I know now is partial and incomplete, but then I will know everything completely, just as God knows me completely.
(1 Corinthians 13:11-12)

In my last year of high school, I finally got diagnosed with "non-specific" colitis. It was the inflammation of the colon, but they didn't know what caused it. Because it was not ulceritic colitis, they didn't look into it much further, but I was constantly in pain. I tried hard to learn what set it off, and what foods to eat and what not to eat, but it was hard. I just suffered through.

My mom told me that I had stomach issues for years. As a child, I would complain about an upset stomach constantly. I remember being in about grade 2 and being so stressed out, to the point of physical sickness. I became the kid who got stuck at the front of the bus with a barf bucket forever.

As it turns out many years later, after an anxiety and depression diagnosis, postpartum depression, etc. I was finally given an ADHD diagnosis in my mid-thirties, which explained a lot. As a child, everything felt like a struggle, and years later, I was watching my own child struggling with the exact same issues.

The issues with feeling misunderstood and never feeling good enough made daily life difficult. Harder than it should have been for a "normal child". After many years of suffering, now looking back, I am pretty certain that stress, being over-prescribed antibiotics as a sickly, misdiagnosed ADHD child may have caused my colitis, and finally led to fixing the root of the problems.

Along with the constant need for stimulation, yet completely overstimulated, the fixation on perfection led me to the point of panic and actual illness. I felt really uncomfortable in my own skin.

Naming and acknowledging my struggle was actually a huge part in connecting the dots, and beginning to heal all the mistruths I had come to believe about myself as a kid, and it was important to me to understand and learn how to manage this inconvenient hurdle, yet also accept it as somewhat of a super power, when harnessed.

I wish I had a more positive outlook as a child; it never made sense to me how a grade 2 child could possibly be that stressed, but it was just part of who I was. It seemed that while I never got to the root of my health issues as a child, anxiety was something that I always had dealt with.

But when it morphed into depression, my faith in God was truly questioned, for the first of many times. It felt like my whole life was a desperate search for what was wrong with me.

The first memories of being sick started around 3-4 years old. The memories included allergy tests, numerous doctor appointments, numerous tests, and notably, the trauma of having to eat my Cheerios with water instead of milk while listening to Enya- Ornica Flow. Sail away. Sail away.

Music has always been a part of me, but it was over 30 years later when I realized "Sail Away" is the name of a song that a lady wrote- a song about the loss of a child. My dad wrote the music to her song. You never know what things link life together.

> **God saved you by His grace when you believed. And you can't take credit for this; it is a gift from God. Salvation is not a reward for good things we have done, so none of us can boast about it. For we are God's masterpieces. He created us anew in Christ Jesus so we can do the good things he planned for us long ago.**
> (Ephesians 3:8-10)

I thought I had a pretty strong faith in God; of course, I didn't comprehend it all, and that is undeniably normal. What might not have been normal is my perception that I needed to have all my ducks in a row and have it all understood.

I certainly didn't feel like a masterpiece, and though I tried my hardest to earn my reward by requiring perfection out of myself, it just wasn't attainable.

I felt pretty confused, because while I loved Jesus as a kid, I didn't truly understand what a gift I had at my fingertips. He loved me, just the way I am.

Rather, I continued to work to try and earn my reward, hoping for at least a participation medal. I could memorize a Bible verse, but did not allow myself to acknowledge there were things I really did not understand.

So while I was busy trying to be the perfect kid, I also had some unrealistic expectations of God. In my mind, I thought it was more of a give and take relationship. "If I do this, could you do this for me?"

Ask and it will be given to you; seek and you will find; knock and it will be given to you. For everyone who asks receives, and the one who seeks finds, and the one who knocks it will be opened.
(Matthew 7:7)

I wanted a life of ease and answered prayer; I'm sure I'm not the only one to think like this. I liked all the promises of the Bible. They sounded like everything would work out, and everyone would get along and be kind and this perfect, utopian dream. I mean, that was the original plan, right?

Unfortunately, those lessons would need to be learned the hard way, as this was the only way a lesson could really stick in my mind. My ideas of how God operated were naïve and, to be honest, restricting. He was in a neat little box, not unlike the genie in a bottle.

I failed to notice the actions I was required to take. I had to ask. Easy enough. But I also had to seek. Ok, I'm looking around... *And* I had to knock. Wait... Where? What door? God's house?

While it all seemed so simple on the surface, turns out it is not as easy-peasy as one might hope. But think about it. The reality of doing these things- asking, seeking and knocking- what does it really look like in real life?

Asking, yes, that's admittedly the easy part. When I was young, I really believed that God answered all prayers, but I believed He would answer in the way I wanted it to happen.

I still deeply believe He does answer all our prayers, but unfortunately, it was a little bit early in my understanding to realize that sometimes the answer is not always a resounding yes, but often it is a no or a not yet.

But seeking, searching, looking; that's where it gets deeper on the scale of personal involvement. What are you looking for? Are you pouring through the Bible, learning about God and looking to understand the things He values in life; the things He wants for you?

Are you searching to understand His desire for your life? Do you look to understand Him enough to know what the right path is compared to the wrong path?

Jesus taught us The Lord's Prayer, and I'm sure most people have at least heard it before.

> **Pray like this:**
> **Our Father in Heaven,**
> **May Your name be kept holy.**
> **May Your Kingdom come soon.**
> **May Your will be done on earth as it is in heaven.**
> **Give us today the food we need, and forgive us our sins,**
> **as we have forgiven those who sin against us.**
> **And don't let us yield to temptation,**
> **but rescue us from the evil one.**
> (Matthew 6:9-13)

Knocking. First of all, are you knocking on the right doors? This means patiently waiting for the doors to be answered and then opened, and then let in. We need to make sure what we are asking for lines up with whatever God's will is. How do we know this? We can trust that if we ask, and it's His will, the right doors open for us and we will be let in.

Sometimes He says no, even if the things we are asking for are really good things. If we want children or a spouse, it's not because wanting that is bad.

He does love blessing us with good things and a good life, but only He knows our hearts motives. It becomes tricky when you want children or a spouse more than you want Jesus.

What are you trying to gain by your prayers? If we are expecting our prayers to be answered, then we need to be aligned with God and knocking on heaven's door with a heavenly perspective on whatever we are asking for. We can never tell God what to do. Try it. He will humble you.

> **Then Jesus said to his disciples** (*followers*)**, "If any of you wants to be my follower, you must give up your own way, take up your cross, and follow me. If you try to hang on to your life, you will lose it. But if you give up your life for me, you will save it. And what do you benefit if you gain the whole world but lose your own soul? Is anything worth more than your own soul?"**
> (Matthew 16:24-27)

Most just want the life of ease. But God never promised that to us. When you start knocking at doors, asking for things that line up with God's plan, that's when commitment comes in.

So while we are praying for the winning lottery number, we are told that we actually need to give up the things we want to truly follow Jesus. So if we are praying for certain things that just aren't in His plan for us, we also need to give up that control we cling to. **Thy will be done.**

If we are on the same page with God, we also must listen to what He tells us we need to *do*. And that's where it becomes a lot more complicated. It is not because He wants anything bad for us. It is because He wants even better.

"My thoughts are nothing like your thoughts," says the Lord. "And my ways are far beyond anything you could imagine. For just as the heavens are higher than the earth, so my ways are higher than your ways, and my thoughts higher than your thoughts.
(Isaiah 55:8-9)

If losing everything, meant you could fully experience God, and I mean, *everything*, would you chose that?

No one likes losing, especially things we feel entitled to. Like a decent life. Health. Family. Friends.

My first experiences with loss and death were life shattering, figuratively and literally. But in all of this, through all my prayers and tears, I was told to pick up my cross, my burdens and my suffering, and to follow Him.

My burdens were heavy. I bore a lot of shame and guilt and sadness, which unless I let go of, it would sink me into bitterness and despair. I most certainly have had seasons in life like that. It held me back, it threatened to sink me, time and time again. Unless I listened to that last line, I would have been still carrying that burden.

But He says to follow him. That will lead to something so good. It's a promise in the Bible. Because of the cross Jesus went to, and because of His death, He led us out of our darkest places.

Then Jesus said, "Come to me, all of you who are weary and carry heavy burdens, and I will give you rest. Take my yoke upon you. Let me teach you, because I am humble and gentle at heart, and you will find rest for your souls. For my yoke is easy to bear, and the burden I give you is light."
(Matthew 11:28-30)

I had a picture come to my mind one day, years after this tragedy took place of a yoke- it was this simple wooden cross beam.

While I knew in my head that it was a yoke, I didn't understand what a yoke really was, so I googled it.

Its purpose ties two animals together. It looks restrictive, but it helps share the weight of the heavy, hard work. It helps the animals work together to accomplish a task that what would be an unbearable load if alone.

It also makes it easier for them to be led by its owner. They can then work with each other, rather than going at it on their own.

A yoke is not holding you back despite its appearance of control.

It is kind. It helps us. It doesn't take away the work, or the effort it takes to get through the mission. It helps us know we are not alone. We are never left alone in this life. God is so good, and so kind, and wants you to know that you are so loved.

The Lord says, "I will guide you along the best pathway for your life. I will advise you and watch over you. Do not be like a senseless horse or mule that needs a bit and bridle to keep it under control" Many sorrows come to the wicked, but unfailing love surrounds those who trust in God. So rejoice and be glad, all you who obey Him. Shout for joy, all you whose heart is pure!
(Psalm 32:8-11)

Life after Death

A family that was close to my family had a little girl by the name of Rachel. She was the sweetest girl, and she got really sick. I wrote about her every day in my diary for over a year, praying daily that she would get better; that God would heal her. I truly believed that Jesus would heal her, in the deepest depths of my heart.

> **"For truly, I say to you, if you have faith like a grain of mustard seed, you will say to this mountain, 'Move from here to there,' and it will move, and nothing will be impossible for you."**
> (Matthew 17:20)

Well, a mustard seed isn't very big, and mountains do move. I thought I had the faith the size of at least a mustard seed on this one. Yet, she never did get well. She was seven years old when she died. It broke my heart, and I began to seriously question everything I thought I believed about God.

She had so much of life ahead. Why did this happen? Why do we exist? What was the purpose?

It was too much for me then. I had dealt with the feelings of being overwhelmed by daily life, but it all became too much for me. It was the first time that I really wondered why I was even alive.

I thought about death a lot, and not only because I was dealing with the deaths of these people that were no longer in my life. It was because I was constantly thinking of the futility of life; questioning "Why?"

As far as I was concerned, there wasn't much of a reason. Everything in me *just hurt*. I have a beautiful little music box Rachel's mother gave me- a piano shaped music box. It was a small reminder of her beautiful life, and it took until just recently to realize the significance of this.

As I grew up, I cherished the piano music box, but I had hid it away for a lot of years to keep it safe. My son found it once, and in fact, broke it a little. So I hid it even higher to protect its sentimental value.

I only just pulled it out today, and played it for my mom, to figure out what song it played. I didn't recognize it, but it was a tune I've listened to many times over the years when I did pull it out of safe storage.

"We've Only Just Begun" by the Carpenters. A wedding song, my mom told me.

This event in my life was literally the moment that began my search for why. How fitting for the song in the music box to be about a beginning.

That same year, a boy in my class died. He died a horrific death, in a fiery car crash with his parents, leaving behind three other children.

The day before he died, my friend had gotten into a fight with him, spat in his face, and we had kind of laughed about it, because we thought he had asked for it. We never had a chance to say sorry; let alone, to say good bye.

Having an experience like that at such a young age taught me that life is truly unpredictable; an erratic, volatile series of events strewn together to call life here on earth. Hardly perfect.

In fact, it's what my therapist would call childhood trauma. And everyone is searching for healing from that.

I had a lot of guilt and shame that I carried with me because of my last memory of this classmate. Somethings you just can't take back. After that hard life lesson, I did strive to treat others with much more kindness and respect than we had treated that boy the day before his untimely death. You never know what the last words to someone could be.

Sometimes the consequences of our actions are something you have to live with for the rest of your life, large or small.

While those deaths rattled me to the core, I was also preparing myself for yet another death. My wonderful Oma, my mother's mother, was dying that year, as well. She had battled cancer for a long time, and she fought that battle a few times.

Her perspective, while she was dying, was in such contrast to how I was dealing with death. To me, it was as if life was falling apart; being ripped away so unfairly. To her, it was that she looked forward to going to heaven.

Despite living through WW2, literally hiding a Jewish woman and her baby in their home, then uprooting her life after that and moving from The Netherlands to Canada, she lived with so much grace, and she continued to die with so much grace.

And they think only about this life here on earth. But we are citizens of heaven, where the Lord Jesus Christ lives. And we are eagerly waiting for Him to return as our Saviour. He will take our weak mortal bodies and change them into glorious bodies like His own, using the same power with which He will bring everything under His control.
(Philippians 3:19-20)

She took a turn for the worst, and since my dad was away on a business trip that week, my mom and I slept in the same bed that last night to comfort each other. We knew she was dying.

We sang the old hymn, 'How Great Thou Art', and cried, knowing the moment we would have to say goodbye would be soon.

Then sings my soul, my Saviour God to Thee
How great Thou are, how great Thou art

The next morning, we got the call that she had passed away that night. It didn't come as a surprise; we knew that night was our night with her on earth.

But each day the Lord pours his unfailing love
upon me, and through each night I sing His
songs, praying to God who gives me life.
(Psalm 42:8)

My mom taught me something about life that night. Despite the sadness in those moments, we could sing about how good God is because we have the hope that she was gone home to heaven; getting to see Jesus.

My Oma taught me something about death that night. If you have hope of life after death, the pain of death doesn't sting when I could see it was something that she was looking forward to. We knew that she had fought the good fight during her life.

I press on to reach the end of the race and receive the
heavenly prize for which God, through Christ Jesus,
is calling us.
(Philippians 3:14)

Then, because life is like a box of chocolates, three days later after the death of my beloved Oma, I broke my arm while I was babysitting in the church nursery. I broke it when I tried to stand on a church chair, having fun, joking with 4 year olds, telling them I was taller than them (no kidding?!), while babysitting my brother and the little brother of Rachel.

Oh, give me back my joy again,
let the bones you have broken rejoice.
(Psalm 51:8)

This was all in the span of about three months. It was 1998, according to my mom's bible. I was 11-12 years old. Little did I know what life would line up for me, and 25 years later, I would still be searching for the answers to my "Why?".

But I trust in Your unfailing love. I will rejoice because
you have rescued me. I will sing to the Lord
because He is good to me.
(Psalm 13:5-6)

Yet, if we can find the strength to sing through the darkest nights and moments, our lives looks more like the life God had actually intended for us. We can keep looking up and looking forward to the hope of seeing God, living with Him forever after death, with Jesus to thank.

Like the hidden away music box from Rachel, I felt like I had a treasure tucked away inside of me, but I didn't know what it even was. I had it in me. Yet, I knew what I had was important, so I kept it safe, without using it. I tried to numb it.

It took time, but I finally understand the importance of the gift of the music box: music itself. It was a lesson I learned throughout the years. Don't let that music box sit in silence.

Make a joyful noise, no matter the season of life. Every season is so beautiful.

Let all that I am praise the Lord; with my whole heart, I will praise His holy name. Let all that I am praise the Lord; may I never forget the good things he does for me. He redeems me from death and crowns me with love and tender mercies.
(Psalm 103:1-2; 4)

Shipwrecked

Then I realized that my heart was bitter, and I was all torn up inside. I was so foolish and ignorant- I must have seemed like a senseless animal to you. Yet I still belong to you; you hold my right hand. You guide me with your counsel, leading me to glorious destiny. Whom have I in heaven, but you? I desire you more than anything on earth. My health may fail and my spirit may grow weak, but God remains the strength of my heart; He is mine forever.
(Psalm 73:21-26)

As many teens do, especially after all the trials in my childhood, I began suffering from depression and a lack of self-esteem. I was constantly worried about my weight. Looking back at pictures, I must have been about 85 pounds, soaking wet, but the image in the mirror only showed my flaws. I convinced myself I was fat; worthless.

As I came to realize, this can be a by-product of ADHD; when a life feels so out of control, this is often a way to feel and element of control over one's life, however unhealthy and harmful.

I began struggling with bulimia, and that was my secret for a few years. Though I recovered from this on my own, I can only imagine the damage this did to my body. I lived my teen years in a fog- a deep, dark fog of utter despair.

I didn't want to be struggling, but I was weak. My faith was as frail as my broken arm bones.

Cling to your faith in Christ, and keep your conscience clear. For some people have deliberately violated their consciences; as a result their faith has been shipwrecked.
(1 Timothy 1:19)

In Alberta, high school starts at grade ten, and the small Christian school I had gone to my whole life only went from kindergarten to grade nine. This meant starting at a new school, so for my first year of high school, I went to a different school in a neighbouring town.

Even though I was new there, I had a lot of friends there already. I suppose I was even popular. With popularity comes drama, and I was never interested in drama. In truth, I couldn't handle much drama, if any. My mind was dramatic enough.

A girl on my two hour bus ride to and from school made my life pretty miserable. We even shared a bus stop, since we lived close together. This made for a long bus ride that year.

It wasn't that fun getting mistreated, but I just tried to ignore it and just listened to my Discman, as loud as possible. For some reason I didn't really care what she thought of me, but my breaking point was when she started making fun of my best friend. I said (ok, yelled) some choice words to her, and she cried the rest of the bus ride home.

It's ironic how the ones that attack others are actually the most insecure. It was obvious and sad as to what was happening. People try breaking others down in an attempt to make themselves feel better, yet this is actually the weakness and insecurity showing in themselves.

I will also point out, my own lesson of speaking with only kindness was clearly not learned at this point in my life, as shown in my impulsivity in my negative speech.

It's really hard to watch your mouth when you feel attacked. These are lifelong lessons that I'm still learning. I am doing my best.

Indeed, we all make mistakes. For if we could control our tongues, we would be perfect and could also control ourselves in every other way.
(James 3:2)

As much as I knew that the bullying would likely subside after I stood up to her, I decided to switch schools after my first year of high school, opting to go to the local public school, after eleven years of going to Christian schools.

It was a hard choice, as I liked most of the people, but there were definitely things I wasn't happy about at that first high school. I felt stifled by the rules, and didn't feel like I fit into the box that was expected of me there. It was a good choice. I had no mortal teenage enemies at my new school, for starters.

Hot and Cold

At the new high school, I didn't have many friends, for the first year in my life. My best friend who was a year younger, started at that high school this same year.

Since it was my first year at this new school, but my second year of high school, and my only friend was in grade ten, most of the people in my own grade just ignored me.

They might have thought I was just a smart grade ten kid who somehow made it into grade eleven classes. Summer school, I guess, could have been a plausible explanation for their assumption.

I went from knowing everyone in my school to suddenly being totally unknown. I lost a lot of confidence, and I suddenly suffered from an incredible shyness, which I had never experienced before. Everyone intimidated me. I hardly spoke that year. I already had self-esteem issues and a sense of unworthiness, which only seemed to grow.

Or maybe it was that I didn't want to get involved in the drama that happens when you are popular. After getting bullied, getting on anyone's bad side stressed me out. I'd rather not be on any side of anyone. I would rather be invisible than getting singled out. Instead, I just tried being friends with everyone. I liked it better that way.

So that year, I mostly made friends with other new kids, the kids who probably felt as out of place as I did. In honesty, I loved all the people I hung out with.

Everyone was accepted for who they were, and we did wild things that all the [undiagnosed] ADHD kids thought were normal like eating hot sauce that made noses bleed, going to punk concerts and generally just trying our best to have a good time.

Also, in my grade 11 year, I got involved with Young Life, a great organization for high school kids across the nation. It was a fun, healthy alternative to the traditional church youth group. It was so accepting. This was how church was meant to look.

It was a new thing in our town, and the bonus was I got to stay connected with my friends from the first high school I went to. We sang songs, and watched the leaders do funny skits, and went tobogganing on couches equipped with skis, even tried to summit a mountain. We had fun. We created deep bonds, unrelenting friendships over the years, despite time in between.

The girl who led the Young Life group in our town was awesome, and she really took me under wing. It was cool to get invited over for lunch at her house. It was one less lunch hour to worry about feeling out of place or lonely.

We also started a Bible study with her, and we studied the book of James. I still appreciate that study, and it is one of my favourite books in the Bible, to this day. I've had lots of those lifelong lessons engrained in my soul from that book.

"How do you know what your life will look like tomorrow? Your life is like a morning fog- it's here a while, then it's gone. What you ought to say is, "If the Lord wants us to, we will live and do this or that."
(James 4:14-15)

That verse brought some healing to my previous pain, like when I had prayed for so long about that little girl who died too young, and when that classmate died, again too young.

I had repeatedly questioned, how could God let something like that happen? I held onto a lot of pain over the years, and that held me back from experiencing a lot of joy in my life.

In my mind, God, who is supposed to literally be a God of love, should not allow pain in my life. However, I'm not God, and I was searching to trying to gain some understanding.

Oh how great are God's riches and wisdom and knowledge! How impossible it is for us to understand His decisions and His ways! For who knows the Lord's thoughts? Who knows enough to give Him advice?
(Romans 11:33-34)

Life was finally starting to feel better for me. I had settled into a good group of friends who liked me for being me, and I had gone from feeling so unworthy of love, to finding some acceptance.

I finally received some help from teachers, who realized some of my struggles, especially with math. I was starting to accept that I was good enough, and didn't need to be as perfect as I had originally planned.

However, after yet another tragic death of a friend, I felt I was at my breaking point when it came to my internal pain. I took it upon myself to finally go to the doctor. I knew the things going on inside my head were not right; it hadn't right been for years. I was always sad. I couldn't shake it.

The doctor gave me a trial sample of anti-depressants, which I never ended up taking. I was told to say no to drugs; that I just needed to deal with my issues and to pray about it.

I often wonder if I had started taking the medications back then, if my life would have had some slightly different outcomes. I continued trying to deal with my pain- physical and mental pain- in whatever way I could, without having access to very effective resources at the time.

Awareness about mental illness has come a long way since then, but there is still so much to learn. Ah, the fight against stigma… The fight against the appearance of having it all together for the sake of saving face.

I spent a lot of years recently talking to people in the church about mental illness. I don't know if the previous generation of church goers valued excellence over vulnerability. It felt that way and left me so confused.

The conversation seemed to focus on how to *be good* rather than how to overcome the moments when things were not good. Judgment and control felt much more accurate than mercy and joy, and I think that is very off target from what I've learned in the Bible.

I could feel myself drifting in the wrong direction again, and felt very frustrated by the Christian circle, seeing hypocrisy and judgment going rampant, especially when it came to actually helping the broken.

I very much understand why people see the church the way they do. This makes me sad looking back, but the reality is that the church is full of humans.

And as humans, we aren't perfect. The church doesn't always have it right. Some churches forget that they aren't perfect. So I understand that it's pretty easy to judge the church, especially when one sees the church judging.

We are all broken. And as it turns out, *we* are the church. Some see the church as people who have it all figured out, when in fact it is exactly the opposite. It's the people who have admitted they don't have it all figured out.

We are the church; all of us, a whole group of imperfect people who decided we can't do it without Jesus.

But the purpose of the church is to build each other up in love, encouragement and praise, joy and thankfulness.

But when the Pharisees (teachers) saw this, they asked his disciples (followers) "Why does your teacher eat with such scum?" When Jesus heard this, he said, "Healthy people don't need a doctor- sick people do." Then He added, "Now go and learn the meaning of this Scripture: 'I want to show you mercy, not offer sacrifices.' For I have come to call not those who think they are righteous, but those who know they are sinners."
(Matthew 9:11-13)

Death Path

The ropes of death entangled me; floods of destruction swept over me. The grave wrapped its ropes around me; death laid a trap in my path. But in my distress I cried out to the Lord; yes, I prayed to my God for help. He heard me from His sanctuary; my cry reached his ears.
(Psalm 18:4-6)

I can probably say, my issues with alcohol began the very first time I got drunk. My family never drank alcohol, at all. With the exception of the one time, at age eight that my dad's friend let me have a sip of his beer, I had never had an alcoholic beverage. I think my dad let him do that to scare me off alcohol. It was pretty disgusting anyways, to an eight year old.

In total honesty, getting drunk for the first time wasn't intentional. I was in eleventh grade, and I had gone over to my friend's house to watch a movie, one Sunday afternoon, ironically after church. His older brother offered me a coke, which, admittedly, tasted funny and a little off. I wrote it off as the no name brand "cola" I suppose I should have questioned it, but I was incredibly naïve about drinking. After watching a movie, and a few "really flat yet spicy cokes" later, I was feeling pretty dizzy.

Suddenly, the lazy Sunday afternoon movie turned into a drunk Sunday evening, with me throwing up in anything that had a drain. I don't remember much about the experience, other than looking at myself in a mirror, hating myself, feeling like my head was about to float away and promptly throwing up in the sink.

I didn't drink again for at least a year and a half. And the next time, and the next time, and the next time brought me right back to those old, disgusting feelings.

Yet this was also the beginning of my self-medication, I suppose. Looking back, alcohol and drugs are a very wrong prescription. I am not a doctor, but I can say with certainty, this is not how to heal.

Life progressed, as it inevitably does, and after high school, I decided I wanted to design houses when I grew up, so I took the Architectural Technology program at the Northern Alberta Institute of Technology in Edmonton. It was a good starting block for my career in design, and after graduating, I moved north.

I lived up north for eight months, and even though I had a lot of fun golfing and floating down rivers, my sadness became more apparent and debilitating. I still could not shake the weight of my shame that I felt.

Yet another friend's death occurred and a relationship unraveled. I had put all of my bets on one person, and they let me down. They couldn't fix me, and I couldn't fix myself.

I spent a lot of time driving back and forth from my new home back to my parent's home, typically a five hour trip, with the excuse of needing to clean my dirty laundry at my childhood home rather than a quick drive to the laundry mat.

Mainly, I was trying to escape the sadness and disappointment of where my life was headed. I drove too fast. I did that five hour trip in 3 hours once. In all honesty, I secretly hoped that I would just crash so that my parents wouldn't have to be disappointed in me or blame themselves if I actually did "it". It would be blamed on the roads or my reckless driving.

If suicide ever becomes an enticing option, that is a very bad place. Turn and run from that! Please, for the literal love of God! You are so loved. There is so much hope to be found.

I cried a lot. But the whole time that I had these horrible thoughts, in my heart, I didn't really want to die. Life had to have some sort of purpose. When you are in a self-loathing, pit of despair, finding some sort of purpose, let alone some comfort, is really difficult. But life has unimaginable value.

"What will you gain if I die, if I sink into the grave? Can my dust praise you? Can it tell of your faithfulness? Hear me, Lord, and have mercy on me. Help me, Oh Lord."
(Psalm 30: 9-10)

One night, I found myself in an emergency room, truly wanting to die. I managed to convince the person who brought me in that waiting two hours was long enough, that this was ridiculous, that I was fine, and that I was just overreacting to my sad circumstances at the time.

We went our separate ways, and I could almost watch my life seem to unravel. Every choice I made seemed to spiral myself out of control. I started drinking way too much, and most nights ended in total blackness. The next morning, I somehow always came back to the reality of life, and would make it to work. It was how I always lived my life- pretending everything was just fine. My smiles always hid the pain.

But, I was still alive.

**The way of the godly leads to life;
the path does not lead to death.**
(Proverbs 12:28)

I pray that I will never return to that place, ever. My heart actually hurt from the turmoil that was going on inside me. It took a long time to recover from that. It was not just heart break from a timed out relationship. It was the gut-wrenching pain of the self-hatred I felt about myself. It was the feeling that you would die, without even needing to pull a trigger.

I am exhausted and completely crushed. My groans come from an anguished heart. You know what I long for, Lord; you hear my every sigh. My heart beats wildly, my strength fails, and I am going blind. I am on the verge of collapse; facing constant pain. But I confess my sins; I am deeply sorry for what I have done. Do not abandon me, O Lord. Do not stand at a distance, my God. Come quickly to help me, O Lord my Saviour.
(Psalm 38: 8-10; 17-18; 21-22)

If you ever feel that way, again please, I beg of you, ask for help. God has placed resources in life. Search out the help.

Canada/ United States Suicide Hotline:

1.833.456.4566

Nonetheless, there was always something pulling me towards God. A neighbour in my apartment building mentioned that they went to the Alliance Church, and that I should try it out sometime. So I went, even though I could hear their fighting and screaming through the walls often.

More often than not, God uses the most unlikely people, and it was a gentle reminder to me that it's about our own relationship with God that is what is important; not about the people *in* the church, who are so broken themselves. You really never know who or what God will use- perhaps a T-shirt, perhaps a license plate, maybe a spicy neighbour.

The beauty of God is that He is very gracious. Much more gracious than humans are. I guess that's why we sing Amazing Grace.

My brothers, if anyone among you wanders from the truth and someone brings him back, let him know that whoever brings back a sinner from his wandering will save his soul from death and will cover a multitude of sins.
(James 5:19)

God always kept me putting out these little reminders, that He wanted me to look to Him, using whoever He could, and whatever he could.

As close as I was to rock bottom, I kept pushing back. In my mind, I still wasn't good enough to accept His love. But people were always around me, throughout life, supporting me, and encouraging me.

Little acts of kindness don't go unnoticed, and from the bottom of my heart, I appreciate every single act that has ever been shown to me. From snow blowing neighbours, to care packages and massages, to a simple chai tea delivery. I've been blessed by so much kindness.

I know how loved I feel when this happens, and I love passing on the love. The best part of random acts of kindness is you aren't expecting a thank you. You are hoping it gets shared. That is the point of love- to pass it on and share it with everyone around you!

Let us think of ways to motivate one another to acts of love and good works. And let us not neglect our meeting together, as some people do, but encourage one another, especially now that the day of His return is drawing near.
(Hebrews 10:24-25)

Small Steps

That year, my friend got married, and at her wedding shower, an older lady gave her some life advice, which I fully took to heart. She started off by saying "Love your neighbour as yourself", and went on to simply explain that you will exhaust yourself if you spend your life trying to love everyone, if you don't take the time to love and care for yourself.

It's not a selfish idea. It finally made sense. It's the very reason you need to put the air mask on yourself during a plane crash before you can help anyone else. The whole time I was wallowing in self-pity, feeling sorry for all the wrong that had happened in my relatively good life, I forgot about my own air supply.

Focusing on making other people happy wasn't going to bring me happiness, and in the same breath, I couldn't depend on someone else to make me happy. People will always disappoint other people. It was very liberating to know that I was the one who was in charge of finding my own happiness. It started to make sense.

For the first time in my life, I focused a little bit more on myself. It was just me, myself and I. I had spent so much of my life already trying to please everyone, trying to get everyone to like me; to be proud of me. It's a bit of a catch twenty two, though, because if you don't like yourself, even if others like you and approve of you, it will never be enough.

I knew that I needed to make some big life changes if I was going to survive this life, and as if to prove to this guy who broke my heart that I could move on, I decided I was going to do something awesome.

So I booked a one way ticket to Switzerland. I subsequently had one of the best years of my life. Lessons started falling into place. I had an amazing group of people surrounding myself, and for the first time in my life, I began to understand the importance of loving myself.

Moving to a foreign country, it became quite easy to focus on finding myself as I didn't really know anyone. I was lucky to be able to surround myself with wonderful girls, and a great support group, specifically for au pairs, strangers to the country, brought together by divine appointment.

That support came in the form of an American couple who lived in Switzerland, supporting au pairs in the surrounding area. I was lucky enough to meet them, and through bible studies, and a few therapy sessions, I felt like I finally had my life on track, or at least in the right direction.

I felt like I began the journey to finding who I was meant to be. It offered me some healing in my disappointments in the church, and while I felt I had found the missing piece, I continued to resist healing and acceptance of meaningful change. With the beauty of nature all around me, I was so blind.

I read a lot when I was in Switzerland, and a quote from the book, Memoirs of a Geisha stood out to me.

> *"We all know that a winter scene, though it may be covered over one day, with even the trees dressed in shawls of snow, will be unrecognizable the following spring. Yet I had never imagined that such a thing could occur within our very selves."*

As a Canadian, I could definitely picture this winter scene the author was speaking of. I was ready for that change.

My whole being wanted to be someone unrecognizable, someone different from who I currently was.

I wanted to be happy. I wanted to love myself. I felt I was in a season where I felt like I was making progress, but I continued to take a step forward, only to take three steps back.

Again, God was whispering to me to accept His love. He was trying to show me and to give to me: His unconditional love.

My second journal entry after arriving in Switzerland read,

*"I still can't believe how happy I am being here. It is so gorgeous.
And I can't believe how everything came together. It was exactly
what I needed in my life. I've never really been happy where
I was; I always felt the need to run away from my problems.
Now that I've really gotten away, I feel like I can deal with my
insecurities and fix those problems that I thought I might not be
able to. Maybe after this, I'll be able to be happy anywhere."*

The big life lesson of loving the person I am was to be learned over the coming years, but Switzerland was where it started for me. Because no one knew me, frankly, I didn't care if people liked me, because I was surrounded by strangers. And because I was surrounded by strangers, I felt that I could be myself.

As it turned out, the strangers in my life liked me, and quickly we went from being strangers, to becoming friends. Really, really good friends!

"…I'm so thankful for friendship. It beautifies life so much."
— L.M. Montgomery, Anne of Avonlea

God puts specific people in our lives; sometimes only for a season. I really do believe that the people He places in our lives are there for a reason.

Sometimes it's to help us grow, sometimes it's to comfort us, and sometimes it's to just have fun and laughter. But the people we keep around us in life is important, whether for good or not.

It was the first time I had ever had a tight knit group of girl friends, and while we all went our own ways after that year in Switzerland, those friends will always be in my heart. They were such a big part of my life. Just because time passes, those friendships don't disappear.

Years later would I experience this type of friendship again, but the next time it would be in a church family, and I am so thankful to have found that acceptance again.

All the while, God kept reminding me of his faithfulness, and it was something I couldn't entirely dismiss. I did believe there was something more, and never completely gave up on my faith in God, thanks to the people that God kept placing in my life.

I'm not sure if it was my own faith at this point, but I did believe that God had something more planned for my life than I could even comprehend. Something big.

"For I know the plans I have for you," says the Lord. "They are plans for good and not for disaster, to give you a future and a hope. In those days, when you pray, I will listen. If you look for me whole heartedly, you will find me. I will be found by you," says the Lord. "I will end your captivity and restore your fortunes."
(Jeremiah 29:11-14)

God is a God of promises. He wants to give good things. He also loves teaching us, and turning us into the people we are meant to be. That is a lifelong journey, and promises are often something we hold onto with hope.

It takes patience and endurance for a lot of His promises, but God's timing is always perfect.

However, God's biggest promise is that He has come to rescue us, and He did that already by Jesus's life here on earth. And He did it symbolically and literally with His death, and the importance of Him coming back to life.

That promise can be accepted at any point in your life. It's your choice to accept that promise or not, but it's certainly not something you need to wait for. If He can raise the dead, He can certainly grant promises.

That is a promise that can be immediately gratified the moment you say yes!

Looking

When I moved back from Switzerland, I really felt the need to be in a place that I loved. I loved Switzerland, and I knew I was looking for something similar. That led me on a journey of figuring out where exactly I wanted to live.

The world was my figurative oyster. I just knew I wanted to be in my happy place. Canada. Home. Mountains. I loved being surrounded by beauty and so close to nature. That was how I landed in Lake Louise- one of the most beautiful places in Canada, if not the world.

After living in Lake Louise for about a year and a half, yet another toxic relationship took me another few steps backwards in my attempts to head in a forward direction. I found myself desperately trying to escape again.

I knew that I needed to get out of the dark place I was in, but since I had already pulled the "move to a foreign country" card, I knew I was needing a place to try to settle my roots.

I couldn't keep running away from my problems forever, mainly since I was my own biggest problem. I traded one set of mountains for another set of mountains, packed up all my stuff and moved to Revelstoke; not really knowing anyone, but hoping for another completely fresh start.

"For the mountains may move and the hills disappear,
but even then my faithful love for you will remain.
My covenant of blessing will never be broken,"
says the Lord, who has compassion on you.

"Oh afflicted one, storm-tossed and not comforted, behold, I will set your stones in antimony, and lay your foundations with sapphires."
(Isaiah 54:10-11)

All this time, no matter where I was, there were small reminders, whether it was a book I read or a last minute decision to drive an hour and a half to go to the closest church, there was always a pull to search for something to fill that emptiness.

I knew I needed to stop running every time life got hard. Running away was just such an easy option, but it never seemed to bring me to the things I was searching for. It was just a change of scenery. Yet, it was the only way I knew how to deal with my problems- pretending they didn't exist.

After making the decision to leave a toxic environment, I was nowhere near where I wanted to be. I was still incredibly storm-tossed. Yet my life's foundation was something to be worked on and I just wanted to get my life on track. I really wanted to lay down some roots.

I was getting really tired of running, trying to find somewhere I could feel like I belonged; somewhere that felt like home. I knew I didn't belong back near my hometown. As much as it was the place that I was born and raised, it had never felt like home to me, even when I was there. I never felt like it was where I belonged.

I always found myself attracted to the mountains, and being in Switzerland only amplified that for me. Which had brought me to Calgary (not quite close enough to the mountains, but not bad), Lake Louise (beautiful, but a dark place for me), Revelstoke (close to perfect), Kelowna (no), and back to Revelstoke (confirmed as close enough to perfection for me).

Revelstoke is an awesome little community. It offered everything I wanted from life. Mountains, snowboarding, an accepting community, unlimited access to beauty...

I was checking all the boxes on my life's wish list, but I was still so empty inside. I couldn't figure it out. After a mental breakdown, I finally went back to the doctor to get some antidepressants, and also got referred to the local mental health unit. I spent a lot of time learning about ways to cope with my depression and anxiety.

I've always been one to learn my lessons the really hard way, and I never seemed to be able to connect the dots. Even though I was making some progress in my personal journey, I still felt an incredible emptiness inside.

But then I will win her back once again. I will lead her into the desert and speak tenderly to her there. I will return her vineyards to her and transform the Valley of Trouble into a gateway of hope. I will make you my wife forever, showing you righteousness and justice, unfailing love and compassion. I will be faithful to you and make you mine, and you will finally know me as the Lord. "In that day, I will answer." says the Lord.
(Hosea 2:14-15; 19-21)

My struggle with drinking continued, as if I was trying to fill myself and that ever-present emptiness with a temporary sense of joy.

There was drama, regrets and awkward circumstances that make life feel like such a waste. I was looking to go in the right direction, but I was still in no place where I should be handed back some vineyards.

Plain and simple, but not easy to accept: alcohol is a depressant, and it just makes things worse when used as an antidepressant. It's clearly impossible to self-medicate depression with a depressant. I always knew I wanted to drink less, as I would feel completely brutal the next day, but I would continue the cycle.

As I learned more about myself and the basic needs of humans, I discovered the importance of focusing on the basics. And it is a good place to start looking for contentment.

We can complicate life as much as we want, but at the end of the day, it really is simple. We have our basic needs: Food, Shelter, and Community. Nice little triangle. Without one point, we can't survive. We need that little triangle to be whole.

Food was easy; I love food. I certainly had shelter, but I felt like I needed to figure out community. I found I had been running away from my problems for so long and pushing people away, I didn't know how to let people help me or how to actually deal with my problems.

After going through a sexual assault and subsequently, a, extremely toxic relationship, I had such a twisted idea of what love looked like. Yet, I wanted so desperately to be loved and accepted that I kept looking to people to give me the deep love I so desperately craved.

Yet I couldn't trust anyone with my already broken heart, I was so fearful of making the same mistakes, as I always seemed to do. All I felt was unworthiness.

I was left in a place where I didn't believe I was loveable anymore; that I was unworthy of any type of love. Looking back, I lament on why I put myself through it all. I was so broken still and unable to take responsibility for myself, my actions, and my life.

Nothing was able to fill my emptiness. I was so hurt from things in my past and my own lack of forgiveness to those who had hurt me that I found myself in a cycle of hurting others to protect my heart from the very connection I was actually hoping for.

That emptiness continued to haunt me, and I felt myself searching for something to fill the emptiness my soul felt, but unsure of what it really was. I was getting so frustrated with myself and where my life was headed. I was still drinking too much; I was in a cycle that I couldn't overcome. I wanted to do it so badly on my own, yet I couldn't trust others, and I couldn't trust myself.

However, we are not meant to live life alone, or to figure it out on our own. We are designed to have friends, family, community, and as I began to finally understand, we are designed to love and to be loved.

I knew deeply that I couldn't do it alone. I knew I needed to trust in something, rather, in Someone that I did not understand.

Trust in the Lord with all your heart; do not depend on your own understanding. Seek His will in all you do, and he will show you which path to take.
(Proverbs 3:5-6)

And still, God was there, quietly trying to get my attention. In my desperate search for love, rather than looking at the One who was constantly trying to get my attention, I tried every other option until I was left with nothing; no other place to turn.

"Come let us return to the Lord. He has torn us to pieces, now He will heal us; now He will bandage our wounds. In just a short time He will restore us, so that we may live in His presence. Oh that we might know the Lord! Let us press on to know Him! I want you to show love, not offer sacrifices. I want you to know me."

(Hosea 6:1-3; 6)

Beauty in the Brokenness

As much as I'd love to think of myself as an eternal optimist, it wasn't a matter of looking at it as thinking the glass half full; my glass was shattered.

Years ago, a friend posted a picture of a broken bowl that had been smashed. He carefully repaired the broken vase with a Japanese technique called "wabi-sabi"- literally using gold to glue the broken pieces of the shattered bowl back together. The reflected act of repairing and effort struck me.

The path of life has broken me time and time again. I didn't always appreciate the direction it has taken me. Yet the journey was to make something beautiful from total brokenness.

I never would have expected to get to a point in life where I can embrace the fact that if I hadn't been sexually assaulted, I would never be able to accurately relate to others who have gone through the same thing or something similar.

Not that I would have wished to go through any of that, it unfortunately happened. Instead of wishing that it never happened, I've learned a lot about enduring adversities. Now in reality, I'm actually thankful that I've been able to be there for a lot of different people who have gone through similar circumstances.

I have seen time and time again where my pain and the lessons I have learned have been able to help someone else process and begin to heal on their own journey.

It's not a pretty conversation to have; it's full of a lot of sadness, pain, regret and shame, but since I've been able to talk a lot about healing and forgiveness, I have found I am not alone.

I've had a lot of conversations with an incredible amount of vulnerability and trust on both sides, and what I've come to see is that they've always taught me understanding from what we've all learned on our journeys. I have learned so much from these connections that otherwise might not be there.

A lot of people have it way worse than the situation I went through. They may still be living the abuse, daily. I don't know exactly how people feel with those incredibly hard situations, but I have an idea now. While not minimizing anyone's experience, there is so much value in gaining understanding through other's experience.

While we may have had someone else's choices forced upon us; like rape, abuse, bullying- whatever it looks like; we always have the choice of how it affects us. What do we do with it? What good could possibly come out of it? Well, what does joy look like without suffering?

> Say to those with fearful hearts, "Be strong and do not fear, for your God is coming to destroy your enemies. He is coming to save you." And when he comes, He will open the eyes of the blind and unplug the ears of the deaf...
> Those who have been ransomed by the Lord will return. They will enter Jerusalem singing, crowned with everlasting joy. Sorrow and mourning will disappear and they will be filled with joy and gladness.
> (Isaiah 35:4-5; 10)

I'd like to say that I've come to terms with what happened to me, but I'm not sure anyone can ever truly get over the violation of your body.

It's not something that ever goes away, like an internal scar that can become infected at any time, if you don't try to continually heal it. If left, you will suffer the subsequent trauma of the old wounds. After some time, acceptance, therapy and learning about myself, I've come to understand perspective on it, but it's always there.

After going through a situation where someone forces their own desires upon you, taking away your own free will, it changed the picture for me and added an element of importance as to why God put a forbidden fruit tree in the Garden of Eden.

This was the start of the war between life and death. Good and evil. God said if you do this, you'll die. Satan says, 'Surely you won't die…'; 'immediately…' he adds under his breath. This was his first attempt at a masterpiece of lies and deception.

But God is so much more powerful, and it's because we were given free will that He has allowed us to have the control we want over our lives. We don't have to love God. We don't have to accept His love. It's always there, but He will never force it upon us. Unfortunately, the right choices are not always made. **But it's always our choice.**

Today I have given you the choice between life and death, between blessing and curses. Now I call on heaven and earth to witness the choice you make. Oh, that you would choose life, so that you and your descendants might live!
(Deuteronomy 30:19)

As much as we can't always control what happens to us in our lives, we have an element of responsibility with what to do with the aftermath; with what life has handed out to us. We have a lot of information about the promises of how our life will work out if we do or don't listen to God.

It's our choice of what to focus on: the pain or the joy. The hurt or the healing. The hate or the love. The death or the life.

We are given an invitation to healing and restoration. We have someone who is interested in saving our lives because we are loved.

Amazing Grace

Finally, the time came for me to give up alcohol, which was something that was definitely holding me back from any sort of meaningful healing.

I got pregnant. Game changer!

Despite my broken life and broken heart, it was in the very second that I found out that I was growing a child inside of my body, that I had found some sense of purpose and responsibility for myself and this child.

Because I clearly had not given myself the love that I now know I deserve, it was a moment in life that I finally something other than myself to live for. It was certainly something to wake me up from my self-loathing and helped me to get off the death path that my self-sabotaging, if not suicidal, lifestyle had me on.

Don't get me wrong, I was scared beyond belief and did not think I was responsible enough to care for another's life when my own was in such chaos. I was too young. I was not ready for this.

Life was not looking how I expected it to look at this point, but a huge decision was made to place my baby's life ahead of my own. I started to clean my life up, making decisions that I hoped would be best for my child and our future as a family.

As hard as I had tried to find my own fulfillment in life, it never felt quite right. Even while I was hating myself, feeling unworthy of anything resembling goodness, I still had a selfish attitude because at the end of the day, I only cared about myself.

But it did give me a fresh outlook on life, and a new chapter in my life. A new beginning, if you will. When I found out there was another life in my belly, my life became about someone else. My world was more than just me now. It became about loving someone else. I finally surrendered, waving my white flag.

My plans had all failed. I had disappointed a lot of people, and there was nothing left in me. I had to surrender. This was out of my hands, and I promptly placed it right into where it should have been the whole time- in God's hands.

But now, O Lord, you are our Father, we are the clay, and you are our potter; we are all the work of your hand.
(Isaiah 64:8)

As someone who was now growing a baby inside my womb, I not only saw how precious life was, but also how it was to love someone so deeply. If I could love someone so much, especially someone who was being created and formed inside of me, what must it look like for God who I believe created me?

For you formed my inward parts; you knitted me together in my mother's womb. I praise you, for I am fearfully and wonderfully made. Wonderful are your works; my soul knows it very well.
(Psalms 139:13-14)

There is something about loving someone else that you are literally forming in the womb- it inevitably and deeply changes you. I began to understand that my parents loved me. If this is the love I feel for the baby growing inside of me, this must be what they were feeling.

I was lucky enough to have good parents. Despite this fact, I still struggled with the concept of understanding how loved I was. My whole perception of life and love had been so clouded by trauma and death that I failed to recognize I am truly, deeply loved.

I was loved from the moment I was born. I hadn't done anything to deserve or not deserve love. I was simply loved because I existed.

Good parents want what is best for their children. Understanding what parenting actually entailed helped me to understand that while parents make mistakes, they typically are doing the best they can with what they've got. I realized I had really good parents. They deeply loved me, as I deeply loved my child. My relationship with my parents began to heal.

> **You parents- if children ask for a loaf of bread, do you give them a stone instead? Of course not! So if you sinful people know how to give good gifts to your children, how much more will your heavenly Father give good gifts to those who ask Him.**
> (Matthew 7: 9-11)

And if this feeling of love for a child was anything like the love God feels for me, why did I have such a hard time accepting it for myself? It began to make so much sense for me. My parents love for me was a reflection of God the Father's love for me.

Yet God's love was even bigger than that, and that feeling of love I had as a parent was the biggest love I could imagine.

A good parent's love is good, maybe even great, but it's not perfect. But His love is perfect. This was the missing piece in my search for love. I finally realized I was looking for love in the wrong places. The truest, most real love that I was searching for so hard. It wasn't in us. It was only in Him.

Whatever is good and perfect is a gift coming down to us from God our Father, who created the lights in the heavens. He never changes or casts a shifting shadow. He chose to give birth to us by giving us His true word. And we, out of all creation, became His prized possession.
(James 1:17-18)

During my pregnancy, I found myself trying to attend church regularly. Just when I found out about my pregnancy, I went to the other church in town and appreciated that no one knew me. Of course, that was the Sunday the pastor decided we should huddle up into little groups to pray together; I found myself bursting into tears, declaring I was pregnant and needed some prayer. Lots of it.

I was scared. Really scared. I was so young and broken, and my life had been turned upside down. I knew I needed help. And I think I knew where to find it this time.

Over the course of the next few years, my life would change dramatically, with the help of the Higher Being. I was still not the perfect person I wanted to be, but I was learning, and striving to do better. But I knew it wasn't because of me or what I could do. It was because I finally realized it was because I could no longer do it without Jesus.

The week after giving birth, I found myself back at the other church in town, out of convenience; the one where I thought no one knew me, yet I ended up actually recognizing a lot of people who had been placed in my life since the beginning of my pregnancy.

This tied an amazing church together into my life, with a neat little bow. I finally found a community who supported me through good times and bad. I really began my search for understanding God.

I felt so thankful that God hadn't given up on me. He placed me into a group of people who cared and loved me. They accepted me as I am, and welcomed me with open arms. And I loved them right back!

He had placed hope back in my heart and through placing people in my life in my darkest times, I had my light at the end of the tunnel.

**The people who walk in darkness will see
a great light. For those who live in a land
of deep darkness, a light will shine.**
(Isaiah 9:2)

I had hard lessons that I still needed to learn, but as I finally realized just how deeply I needed to surrender my own control and my own fears, when I held my baby boy in my arms, I found myself unable to remember a single nursery rhyme to sing Him. I could only sing Amazing Grace.

**Amazing grace
How sweet the sound
That saved a wretch like me
I once was lost, but now I'm found.
Was blind but now I see.**

Perfecting Love

Feeling truly loved for the first time is not an easy thing to grasp, or accept. Now having my son in my life, giving love came as naturally as maternal instincts are to a new mom. Plus, they are just so cute. How could you not love them? Honestly!

Loving someone else is an easier concept for me. Loving people, other than my son, was still a struggle at times; I had deep resentment I didn't realize I was holding onto.

But accepting love? Allowing yourself to feel love? That was the hardest concept I've ever come to grasp. I was so broken at this point in my life; it's hard to love someone with so much baggage, carrying such complex guilt.

Now I realized that God loved me. He had loved me the whole time, even though I had refused to see it. He truly loved me.

I was some seriously damaged goods. I wasn't even able to love myself, let alone accept the idea of being loved, yet somehow I had an expectation of how I thought I should feel loved and how I should be shown love.

I searched to understand love better, and had read a very good book, which I highly recommend to anyone who wants to understand the logistics of feeling loved and who wants the people around them to feel loved. It's called the Five Love Languages by Gary Chapman.

It relates pretty directly to the type of person you are, whether you are an introvert or extrovert and different elements of how we function. Myers Briggs kind of stuff, but from a love perspective. Basically it's as follows:

Words of Affirmation
Acts of Service
Receiving Gifts
Quality Time
Physical Touch

In it, it simply lays out that we are all very different and that we have different methods of showing love and accepting love. Love is complicated. But it can be learned.

Basically, because I had now discovered love, I wanted to feel more loved, and I wanted to make sure that others in my life felt loved too. I wanted my home to be a home filled with love. While I was certainly trying to do my best, my best would still never be good enough.

My ways of understanding love were still stifled and chaotic in my mind. Love was still surrounded by fear for me. I found myself reverting back to my perfectionistic tendencies, and tried to perfect the art of love. Not so with God.

We would forever be disappointed by love if it were up to fellow humans. Our expectations of perfect, pure love are just not able to be fulfilled by anyone else, regardless of how hard one might try.

Love is very much a choice, not a feeling. Feelings come and go. You can choose to love someone or not. It is always a choice. Take it or leave it. Work at it or don't. It's something you cannot force or control. That is not love.

Everyone's basic need in life is to be loved. I had searched it out for my whole life in all the wrong places. We cannot grasp how to truly love someone else in the way they need, and they will never be able to perfectly love us. We are humans, after all.

There is always an expectation of being loved in return for love. If that type of love was the only love you ever experienced, it would always lead to disappointment.

Have you ever been disappointed by someone you love? Not a nice feeling. Have you ever tried to love someone to only be rejected by that someone after giving everything you had to give? Not pleasant.

> **Oh, how generous and gracious our Lord was! He filled me with the faith and love that comes from Christ Jesus. This is a trustworthy saying, and everyone should accept it: "Christ Jesus came into the world to save sinners"- and <u>I am one of the worst of them all.</u> But God had mercy on me so that Christ Jesus could use me as a prime example of His great patience with even the worst sinners. Then others will realize that they, too, can believe in Him and receive eternal life.**
> (1Timothy 1:14-16)

I can seriously relate to the writer, Paul, here. I felt like the absolute, worst person for a long time, like a person undeserving of love. Maybe we aren't murderers, but we still have hurt people in our lives; we've lied, we've done things we aren't proud of.

Now, I'm not the worst person in the entire world, but when it boils down, I am not perfect, like I want to be. I think everyone wants to be the best they can be. Can anyone say we are perfect? No one is.

> **Jesus told him, "If you want to be perfect, go and sell all your possessions and give the money to the poor, and you will have treasure in heaven. Then come and follow me."**
> (Matthew 19:21)

This was Jesus's answer to a question about what we can do to earn eternal life. His answer points out an impossible task in the question. The rich man who asked Jesus the question walked away sad, because he wasn't able to sacrifice his life of comfort for Jesus's answer to his question. It wasn't possible.

> **Someone came to Jesus with this question: "Teacher, what good deed must I do to have eternal life?"**
> (Matthew 19:16)

So what can we *do* with this impossible task? There are two points in Jesus's answer, and the only thing that we can actually *do*, is to come and follow Him.

> **Then Jesus said to his disciples, "I tell you the truth, it is very hard for a rich person to enter the Kingdom of Heaven. I'll say it again- it is easier for a camel to go through the eye of a needle than for a rich person to enter the Kingdom of God!"**
> (Matthew 19:23-24)

Our reality is confirmed. This is actually impossible for us to do. We cannot earn our salvation, we cannot work our way into heaven. He actually highlights the impossibility of the task, turns the impossible answer around, and He does the part that we cannot do for us.

> **Jesus looked at them intently and said, "Humanly speaking, it is impossible. But with God, all things are possible."**
> (Matthew 19:26)

Wink, wink. This is how Jesus ends His Q&A. With a mike drop.

Knowing full well the impossibility of us being able to *do* what His answer requires, God gives up everything of His. He gives up His only Son for us, because we can't *do* anything.

He becomes the answer to our question. How do we do this if we aren't perfect? Him. Only Him.

God sends His deeply loved Son to die for us, so that we can be something that is impossible for us to accomplish- to be perfect. He loved us so much that we can have our brokenness and shame taken away completely and be forgiven and made perfect. He did the impossible, and made us perfect.

Jesus dies for us so that we, as undeserving as we are, can have a hope that we can live, even after we die. And then God wants to use us, as undeserving as we are, as an example of how awesome He is at giving us grace. Amazing grace.

He personally carried our sins in his body on the cross, so that we can be dead to sin and live for what is right. By his wounds, you are healed.
(1 Peter 2:24)

Just like he said to Matthew, a tax collector, a pretty horrible person, someone who everyone loved to hate,

"Follow me."
(Matthew 9:9)

Come as you are. That's all God wants with us. He wants the broken, the hopeless, the suicidal, those who are ashamed. He accepts us exactly as we are. He loves us, in spite of ourselves.

None of us can say we are exactly who we are supposed to be- we will never be perfect on our own. But we *can* be exactly who we are meant to be.

Even those who aren't as broken as some, we can have all the money in the world, and we are still going to be met with the same fate.

They trust in their wealth and boast of great riches. Yet they cannot redeem themselves from death by paying a ransom to God. Redemption does not come so easily for no one can pay enough to live forever and never see the grave.
(Psalm 49:6-9)

There is nothing that we can do ourselves to be perfect; there is nothing we can do to save ourselves from death. We all have a past. Can we trust that He has a good future for us? All He wants is to love us, and for us to come, take it and follow Him.

He wants to pour His perfect love into our lives and make it right. There is nothing we can do to earn that love, and there is also nothing we can do that will separate us from His love.

And I am convinced that nothing can ever separate us from God's love. Neither death, nor life, neither angels no demons, neither our fears for today or our worries about tomorrow- not even the powers of hell can separate us from God's love. No power in the sky above or in the earth below- indeed, nothing in all creation will ever be able to separate us from the love of God that is revealed to us in Christ Jesus our Lord.
(Romans 8:38-29)

If we are to experience the fullness of life, we need to experience the fullness of perfect, never ending love. He's got it all covered. Turns out He *is* Love. And love is all you need.

We know how much God loves us, and we have put our trust in His love. God is love, and all who live in love, live in God, and God lives in them. And as we live in God, our love grows more perfect. So we will not be afraid on the day of judgement, but we can face Him with confidence because we live like Jesus here in this world.
(1 John 4:16-19)

My son said today as we talked about this book I've been working on for all these years,

"Live a great life. Live a great death."

Yes, because with Jesus, death isn't a true death. It's just your life moving into a different season.

Law + Order

When I began reading the Bible more, I often skipped over the Old Testament, (the part of the Bible written before Jesus aka BC times) because I figured it was more or less irrelevant to me. Jesus had come to the world to change how things were done, so what could I need to know from the older section? Plus, it was confusing.

A lot of it was pretty barbaric in my mind, sacrificing and wars and cruel happenings that I didn't understand. I remember reading about Abraham in Genesis, the earliest book in the Bible, and wondering how God really operated. He asked wild, unimaginable things of people; things that just didn't make much sense.

Abraham is known as the father of many nations, specifically the Jewish generation, through God's promise of a son to Abraham and his wife. Abraham's descendants are historically relevant, even in this day and age.

Wars rage today because of Abraham's descendants. It's right there in Genesis 15-21; it was the start of the division of religions. Abraham's first son went on to bring Muhammed into the world, while Abraham's second son, the son that was promised by God, went on to bring Jesus into the world through the genealogies. Two hugely important historical figures are genetically traced right back to Abraham.

Abraham, the one that God promised to make the father of many nations, didn't even have a son until he was really old-past the age of child bearing age, even back then. Abraham's child, Isaac, was promised to Abraham and his wife, Sarah by

God, and that promise was delivered to the family when they were about 100 years old.

Obviously, Abraham's son was important to him. They had waited years and years to have Isaac, even waiting ten years after God promised to bless Sarah with a baby.

God finally delivered His promise, always in His own time, to Abraham and Sarah, and then in the very next chapter of Genesis, God asks Abraham to sacrifice his own son, the one God promised to him, like an animal sacrifice.

How could God, the God of the New Testament, the God of love ask that of a father? That's a pretty extreme measure for even God to take. How could God ask someone to prove their love for God by killing their very own son?

I remember being so disturbed, trying to understand the point of this story, and thinking, "How dare God ask someone to sacrifice their son." But how could a story like this be relevant in my own life? This is what I would come to know and understand as foreshadowing. Pointing to a future event that was going to be big.

Good news is, God stopped Abraham before he actually killed his own son. It never happened. Thank goodness.

I love my son so much. I can easily say I would die for him, because in a heartbeat I would. I would protect him with my life, absolutely. Chances are, life won't (hopefully) ever put me in a situation where I would need to make that sacrifice; my life for his.

But I would. I will protect him, teach him, nurture him, and help him grow into the person he will become, helping him find his purpose in life. I will answer any questions he has about life and purpose, I want only what's best for him.

On the other hand, I held on to the idea that I would NEVER sacrifice my son's life for anyone else. Not myself. Not anybody.

How dare God ask that of anyone? Children are blessings from God. How could anyone sacrifice their own son?

And that's exactly what God asked of Abraham. Are we able to love God more than our own sons or daughters? God proved His point in stopping Abraham that God would **never** ask us to sacrifice our own children, but He certainly was testing Abraham's faith in how far Abraham's love for God went.

Would we be able to release the control of our children into God's hands? Could I offer my children, could I trust God to know what's best for my children's lives? I needed to be in a place where I could offer my children into the hands of God.

That is the ultimate surrender in life. I needed to trust that God would take care of their lives. All I can do is to pray for them, do my best as a parent to teach them, and trust their lives to God.

Again, God knew exactly what He was asking of Abraham when he asked him to sacrifice his own son. While I was thinking, how dare God ask anyone such a thing, He, Himself, sacrificed His own Son, His only Son, for us. God did the unthinkable, Himself. He knew those feeling of horror would make us think and reflect, 'What is the reality of this act?'

But He was pierced for our rebellion, crushed for our sins. He was beaten so we could be whole. He was whipped so we could be healed. All of us

> like sheep have strayed away. We have left God's
> path to follow our own. Yet the Lord laid
> on him the sins of us all.
> (Isaiah 53:5-6)

But He knew this act would literally mean the fear of death is forever gone. Jesus didn't stay dead. God knew the big picture. But Abraham didn't. Yet he trusted that God would work it out. That's faith.

Imagine sacrificing your son for some stranger, someone who doesn't even care, someone so undeserving. Yet He did just that because He **so loves** us. The heartbreak of God is unimaginable, sacrificing His own Son, whom He loved, because He also loves us. God literally did that for us.

He loves us SO MUCH. Even when we didn't deserve it. When were weren't willing to trust it all to God.

> **When we were utterly helpless, Christ came at just the**
> **right time and died for us sinners. Now, most people**
> **would not be willing to die for an upright person,**
> **though someone might perhaps be willing to die for**
> **a person who is especially good. But God showed His**
> **great love for us by sending Christ to die for us**
> **while we were still sinners.**
> (Romans 5:6-8)

Not only did God send His SON to die, He sent His Son to die for a bunch of broken people who were actually quite happy to see Him die.

We can tell ourselves that it wasn't us who physically killed him. We weren't around back in history when this happened. How could we have possibly done it?

Pilate said to them, "Then what shall I do with Jesus
who is called Christ?" They all said "Let him be
crucified!" And he said, "Why, what evil has he done?"
But they shouted all the more,
"Let him be crucified!"
(Matthew 27:22-23)

God loves us, even when we spit in His face. He loves us
when we reject Him, time and time again. I knew the guilt
of laughing after watching someone spit in someone's face. I
knew the guilt of not being able to say sorry because that boy
died the next day. I cannot make that right.

But we have the chance to accept forgiveness, even though we
do not deserve it. It is being offered to us.

"I tell you, her sins- and they are many- have been
forgiven, so she has shown me much love. But a person
who is forgiven little only shows little love. Then
Jesus said to the woman, "Your sins are forgiven."
(Luke 7:47)

I know I spent a lot of my life, not accepting His love for me.
That is the utter rejection of Him that I participated in. I was
just as guilty as those in the crowd, yelling to kill Him.

I may not have been in the crowd, but my actions and rejection
of His love are just as loud as the shouting in the streets that
historical day, thousands of years ago.

Repent, all who forget Me; I will tear you apart,
and no one will help you. But giving thanks is a
sacrifice that truly honours Me. If you keep my
path, I will reveal to you the salvation of God.
(Psalm 50:22-23)

And He asks for this of us. Apologize. And then, like a meaningful apology, your actions will reflect the change of your ways. Love will change your life in a huge way!

I am not worthy of this gift, this inheritance of eternal life, without accepting the forgiveness offered to me. I cannot do anything to earn something I don't deserve. After a sacrifice like that, giving up His only Son, we are so indebted.

Regardless of how we've been, what we do, Jesus still died for every single one of us. He wanted to have a relationship with us and to love us regardless of how we've acted, how we've treated His offer. We simply need to stop, turn from our own path and accept His perfect love.

Our lives change; not because we are suddenly perfect. We are friends with God. I don't want to intentionally hurt my friends, and I know they don't want to intentionally hurt me. But working at making it right again, with a friend or with yourself.

Mistakes happen. Miscommunications happen. Assumptions happen. But it wouldn't be a very good friendship if you went on intentionally hurting someone. After an apology, things like that change. You strive to do better. To become better, to work through the hard. You do it because you love each other. That's friendship.

Live a life filled with love.

Imitate God, therefore, in everything you do, because you are His dear children. Live a life filled with love, following the example of Christ. He loved us and offered Himself as a sacrifice for us, a pleasing aroma to God.
(Ephesians 5:1-2)

So Loved

How could I have been so oblivious to seeing just how much He loves me?

**"For God <u>so loved</u> the world that he gave his only Son,
that whoever believes in him should not perish,
but have eternal life"**
(John 3:16)

Most people are at least familiar with this passage in the Bible. But please think about what it's really saying; what really happened.

Jesus died in between two people who deserved to die. We deserve to be the ones who were to die. Not Jesus. He took our place. A sacrifice was needed in God's eyes to take away our corruption, the sins of the entire world.

During the journey of accepting God's love, I went through some serious life changing thought processes. If God so loves me, just as I am, I not only had to receive His love, but also His forgiveness.

We are given the choice to live; to really be alive. We are given the choice to enjoy everything we were meant to be, and all we have to do is accept it.

It's something I love to think of as regardless love. No matter who we are, or what we've done, God loves us. He loves us so much, even when we hated Him, he sent us love. **Regardless love.**

God loves me, regardless of who I am, or what I've done in my life. I can be bold and confident in this.

> "This means that anyone who belongs to Christ
> has become a new person. The old life is gone;
> a new life has begun!"
> (2 Corinthians 5:17)

This is pretty awesome news because I could definitely deal with having a new life, suddenly able to be a new creation. We all have something we'd like to change about ourselves, but the opportunity to become a whole new person? Yes, please and thank you.

I know who I am. That took a lot of searching, and it can be defined in my personality, my upbringing, and my ideas. I am perfectly loved, but I am imperfect.

As much as I've learned about myself and tried different techniques to live a happier life, I would be right back to the darkest days of my life, if I wasn't rescued from my old life.

I'm not who I used to be anymore. I don't even recognize the person I was.

> Dear children, let us not merely say that we love
> each other; let us show the truth by our actions. Our
> actions will show that we belong to the truth, so we
> will be confident when we stand before God. Even if
> we feel guilty, God is greater than our feelings, and
> He knows everything. Dear friends, if we don't feel
> guilty, we can come to God with bold confidence.
> (1 John 3:18-21)

I refuse to be stuck in those dark days, I now have a hope that has allowed me to continue on with life, and it has been much more fulfilling. I am able to be a different person because I believe that Jesus loves me.

I could list off everything I've done; everything I feel guilty for, everything I wish I could change. But the past is just that. We cannot change history, but we certainly can learn from it, and try to better ourselves after learning those painful lessons. I've had to make countless apologies to people over the years.

I am truly sorry for the hurt I've caused people. I can't always fix these situations I've caused, but I know I am not the same person I was. I hope my actions reflect that. At the end of the day, we know we are broken beyond human repair.

All of us used to live that way, following the passionate desires and inclinations of our sinful nature. By our very nature we were subject to God's anger, just like everyone else. But God is so rich in mercy, and He loved us so much, that even though we were dead because of our sins, He gave us life when He raised Christ from the dead. (It is only by God's grace that you have been saved!)
(Ephesians 3:3-4)

I still deal with feeling that creep up from the guilt of my shameful past, but I cannot let myself focus on the past anymore, but now and the future. Not when I have the promise that I am a new creation.

Accepting undeserved love and forgiveness is part of who I am to my core, I have come from being a very broken, fragmented person to becoming a person who is fully and perfectly loved by God. I've come to terms with the fact that I will not be perfect on my own.

The reality is we are all winging it. The reality is I am so broken, and that's who I am. We all make mistakes that we aren't proud of, and we will continue to make mistakes. We are human. But this is why we need Jesus, so we can be imperfectly perfect. Beautifully broken.

God has a very clear history of using the most broken to do His work. Not the ones who have it figured out. He rarely used the high priests in the Bible; rarely uses the ones who have it all figured out. It was those people who were hidden in holes (Gideon), prostitutes (Rahab, woman at the well), tax collectors (Matthew, Zacchaeus), servants (Daniel), even murderers (Paul, formerly known as Saul/ King David). Those were the people God chose.

Those certainly aren't the people we probably would pick as *our* first choice. I suppose this is why God is God and we aren't. Although I'm sure our choices may appear to look better, at least on the outside...

The ironic part of God is that if He were to choose a person who is, in our sense, awesome, people would look at it very differently. *Of course, God used them,* they could say. *They are awesome, what would God do without people like that?*

In our world, that would make sense. In our minds, we could make sense of that.

But oh, the reality with God is so very different from that. What would God do with people like me? What could He possibly do?

**But he said to me, "My grace is sufficient for you,
for my power is made perfect in your weakness."**
(2 Corinthians 12:9)

God uses things to emphasize the fact that it is Him working, not us. He will quickly remind you if you become proud about what you think 'you' are doing.

If we were to really believe that, I think the expectations we place on ourselves, predominantly our thoughts that God can only use us when we are perfect, would be very different. He makes the imperfections in us perfect.

The truth really is that God can then use us best when we are willing, despite being broken or our shortcomings or our failures.

God is so opposite of what we think He should be. Everything to us is a confusing, complicated process. It doesn't make sense to us, because God chose to do something that doesn't make sense. He repairs the unrepairable.

Forgiving ourselves should be easy if we are forgiven by God. He made something impossible, possible through His own actions towards us, it became so simple for us. We just need to accept His love and forgiveness, and we become a new creation.

With good news like that; we basically are supposed to be proud of how weak we are, we should embrace our shortcomings. Embrace that, I must.

So now I am glad to boast about my weakness, so that the power of Christ can work through me. That is why I take pleasure in my weakness, and in the insults, hardships, persecutions and troubles that I suffer for Christ, for when I am weak, then I am strong.
(2 Corinthians 12:10)

Simple, but not easy. It's not easy to endure all those things- insults, hardships. It hurts. It's uncomfortable.

But His grace is sufficient for me. His grace is all I need. His love is all I need.

Since you have been raised to new life with Christ, set your sights on the realities of heaven, where Christ sits at God's right hand. Think about the things of heaven, not the things of earth. For you died to this life, and your real life is hidden with Christ in God. And when Christ, who is your life, is revealed to the whole world, you will share in all His glory.
(Colossians 3:1-4)

All we can do is our best, with the help from Jesus. The purpose of accepting God's love is not so that we can live a carefree, sinless life. It is like any relationship- it requires continual work. It has its ups and downs.

We are going to struggle at times, and we are going to live a fulfilled life at times. Some days are better than others, but through Christ's love, we can know that we are doing our best to live our lives as God wants us to live. We can know that while we are not perfect, we are forgiven.

What counts is whether we have been transformed into a new creation. May God's peace and mercy be upon all who live by this principle; they are the new people of God.
(Galatians 6:15-16)

We are a new creation as soon as we accept the fact that God loves us, chains are broken, and we become free from our slavery to sin. Not perfect, but forgiven. And He will forgive us over and over. He's really patient with us. He gives us the time to learn from our mistakes.

A clean slate. A second chance. A new life. Born again.

> **It is no longer I who live, but Christ lives in me. So I live in this earthly body by trusting in the Son of God, who loved me, and gave himself for me. I do not treat the grace of God as meaningless. For if keeping the law could make us right with God, then there would be no need for Christ to die.**
> (Galatians 2:20-21)

The single action of Jesus dying on the cross for us is **exactly** why we need Jesus. If we could "be good enough", we wouldn't need Jesus. But we will never be good enough to make it ourselves to heaven; we can't earn the eternal life that is promised to us because it is a gift to us.

Chain Breaking

**Seek the Lord while you can find Him. Call on Him now
while He is near. Let the wicked change their ways and
banish everything thought of doing wrong. Let them
turn to the Lord that He may have mercy on them. Yes,
turn to our God, and He will forgive you generously.**
(Isaiah 55:6-7)

Forgiving myself for everything that has happened in my
life has not been easy. Letting go of guilt I've carried and the
resentment I've held against myself has been a huge struggle.
It is so easy to blame myself for not being perfect; for not being
wise enough to do something that I knew wasn't right. Yet, it's
not okay to stay in my shame.

If we are feeling fearful because of the shame we carry for
all the bad things we have done, we haven't understood what
God is really all about. Or if we fear that our punishment we
deserve will be to burn in hell, that's not what the Bible says.
God isn't hoping that the world goes down in flames. He does
not want to punish us eternally to the depths of hell.

He is so happy when we figure that out. Even if it takes a long
time for us to figure it out, He wants us to be free from fear.
He wants us to truly understand the reality of His perfect love.

**There is no fear in love, but perfect love casts
out fear. For fear has to do with punishment and
whoever fears has not been perfected in love.**
(1 John 4:18)

This paints a very different picture of God from what
mainstream ideas say. Some people picture God as the ultimate

judge, sitting on a giant throne, who will smite sinners at the first given chance with his trident, spewing fireballs, every time you mess up.

If God is love, that picture must be hugely inaccurate. He wants to save us and He wants us to come to Him so He can rescue us.

We do need Jesus. We need to accept that He loves us and forgives us. This is my truth. This is the truth I hope *you* can have faith in. This is freedom in life.

Isn't that what the world wants? Freedom? We fight wars over it, we stand up for freedom; we fly flags for freedom. The cost of this war was literally paid for with Jesus' life. He wanted to win us back from our slavery so we could become His kids!

**God sent Him to buy freedom for us who were slaves
to the law, so that He could adopt us as His very own
children. And because we are His children, God has sent
the Spirit of His Son into our hearts, prompting us to
call out, "Abba, Father". Now you are no longer a slave
but God's own child. And since you are His child,
God has made you His heir.**
(Galatians 4:5-7)

We cannot do it without God. We will struggle until the day we die. A really good teacher who has his life turned upside down by Jesus, Paul admits his own struggle with sin.

**For I do not understand my own actions. For I do not
do what I want, but I do the very thing I hate.... For I
know that nothing good dwells within me, that is, in my
flesh. For I have the desire to do what is right, but not
the ability to carry it out. For I do not do the good I want,
but the evil I do not want to do is what I keep on doing.**
(Romans 7:15; 18-19)

The biggest realization I had when it came to my imperfections was that God actually wants me to be free from it. He wanted to break me free from addictions and from pain, all those things are brokenness.

We are trapped in our brokenness, slaves to sin, without the rescue from God. God doesn't want us to be slaves to that life anymore. God wants us to "die to our old selves", so that we may start our new life, even though He knows we are unable to be perfect. We are made perfect because He is so full of forgiveness and so much undeserving grace.

Whether it is the chains of addiction, the chains of anxiety, the chains of death, He wants you to be free and perfect in His love.

Now, that isn't an easy task to release the things that hold you trapped. Everyone has their struggles. While we are to be proud of our weakness, we aren't supposed to give into our weakness.

That seems like a contradiction. I think what it means is that, even though we are weak, and we continue to mess up and sin, even though we are trying to **"Go and sin no more."** God knows the impossibility of that.

That is why it is only possible with accepting forgiveness. We really need to ask Jesus for help. Every. Single. Day. Every moment.

We will never experience true freedom here on earth. I really believe that we are on earth for something much more than life. There is life, unimaginable life, just around the corner.

Forgiving ourselves is a huge part of accepting God's forgiveness. It's putting faith in the fact that God has, in fact, forgiven us. He has released us from whatever it is holding us back from freedom in Jesus.

Jesus often told stories to help us to understand. In one of His stories, he talked about sheep. He talks a lot about sheep. Sheep, apparently, aren't very intelligent. This makes it all the more relatable! So it seems very fitting that Jesus would tell a story about sheep.

Even King David, a former shepherd turned king, wrote a poem about how the Lord is my Shephard (Psalm 23); David, of all people, understood what it took to keep sheep safe. Despite us always trying to go our own direction, this way and that way, falling off cliffs and getting eaten by lions, God really wants to protect us, and save us from ourselves.

"What man of you, having a hundred sheep, if he has lost one of them, does not leave the ninety-nine in the open country, and go after the one that is lost, until he finds it? And when he has found it, he lays it on his shoulders, rejoicing. And when he comes home, he calls together his friends and neighbours, saying to them, 'Rejoice with me, for I have found my sheep that was lost.' Just so, I tell you, there will be more joy in heaven over one sinner who repents than over ninety-nine righteous persons who need no repentance"
(Luke 15:4-7)

Picture this: God throws a party every time someone figures out their relationship with Him. How cool is that?

That's the heart of God. God doesn't want to lose anyone. He wants us all to know His love; to be in His family. He isn't interested in sending anyone to hell. He really doesn't. Even when we are caught red-handed.

Take for instance this time a woman was caught in adultery and the morality police brought her straight to Jesus. The people were judging her, and expected Jesus to hand out judgment and wrath out to her.

Here, Jesus, who is perfect in every way, doesn't even condemn a woman who was caught in the act. I doubt they gave her the grace to even get dressed.

Imagine her shame. Her humiliation. The embarrassment. The fear. The actual fear of possible death.

> **"Teacher, "they said to Jesus, "this woman**
> **was caught in adultery. The Law of Moses**
> **says to stone her. What do you say?"**
> **But Jesus stooped down and wrote in the dust with**
> **His finger. They kept demanding an answer so he**
> **stood up again and said to them, "All right, but let the**
> **one who has never sinned throw the first stone!"**
> **Then he stooped down again and wrote in the dust.**
> **When the accusers heard this, they slipped away one**
> **by one, beginning with the oldest until only Jesus was**
> **left in the middle of the crowd with the woman.**
> **Then Jesus stood up again and said to the woman,**
> **"Where are your accusers?**
> **Didn't even one of them condemn you?"**
> **She said, "No one, Lord." And Jesus said,**
> **"Neither do I; go and sin no more"**
> (John 8:7; 10-11)

Jesus, who is God, who has the right to judge the whole world if He wants to, doesn't judge her.

He even gets down, into the dust, and takes the focus off of her, distracts people by writing something, and Jesus used this opportunity to show how serious He is about loving us, not judging us. He wants to rescue us from our chains.

> **Wake up, wake up, O Zion!**
> **Clothe yourself with strength. Put on your**
> **beautiful clothes, O holy city of Jerusalem,**
> **for unclean and godless people**
> **will enter your gates no longer.**
> **Rise from the dust, O Jerusalem.**
> **Sit in a place of honour.**
> **Remove the chains of slavery from your neck,**
> **O captive daughter of Zion.**
> **For this is what the Lord says, "When I sold you into**
> **exile, I received no payment. Now I can redeem you**
> **without having to pay for you.**
> (Isaiah 52:1-3)

The book of Isaiah was written about 400 years before Jesus walked on earth. This was written 400 years before this woman was brought in front of Jesus, and it absolutely reflects what Jesus is doing here.

They caught you in the act, you were trapped in oppression because of your shame. You were excluded, rejected.

You deserve that. That's what we all deserve.

Yet, standing face to face with Jesus, in that moment in time, He wants to buy you out of your captivity. And not with money. His cost was His life, His blood was literally spilled out because that's what we are worth to him. A life for a life. Your life and my life. He came to die so we didn't have to.

No one likes getting judged, but we are definitely quicker to play judge. I would also like to note that the people Jesus was talking to in the story were self-righteous people, people who had no shame in calling out this woman's now very public sin of adultery.

Being the self-righteous people that they were, were they not even able to admit that they were without fault. They would be guilty of lying to themselves if they were to throw that first stone.

Justice requires a payment for debt. But he not only chose to forgive it, rather than to condemn us, but also to pay the debt, even our most public sins. All He wants from us is to **"Go and sin no more."**

Yet, we are paid for. So wake up! Get dressed. Be strong. Become beautiful. Don't let people treat you like you are worthless. Get out of the dust and dirt. Take back your honour and dignity. Take off the chains.

If we are forgiven by Jesus, regardless of what we have done, then why is it so difficult to accept that forgiveness from Him, and to forgive ourselves, and especially, to forgive others?

I've had a very hard time with forgiveness. How can you forgive someone who isn't sorry; someone who hurt someone else so badly? I struggled for years with being unable to forgive the person who sexually assaulted me. He may still be doing it to others, that was truly my motivation in pursuing the assault after seven years, but a big part of me also wanted to have a chance to see him come to some sort of justice.

After going through a lawyer to obtain the information I had requested regarding the assault, I eventually received a letter denying the request. I had already received the file numbers, so I did know that the file existed.

However, being denied the very information regarding my own sexual assault left me feeling very frustrated in the whole system of justice. I wasn't sure what to do at that point, so I began to look inwards instead.

I had let the bitterness of the assault overwhelm my life for seven years at this point. I had come to realize in the following years that self-medicating with alcohol was not working, but only creating more problems in life for me.

There had to be something more. I had to learn how to deal with this, once and for all.

Realizing that I would not be receiving the information I would need to pursue any sort of justice against the person who had done serious wrong to me, a still small voice was telling me to let go.

Without acquiring an official subpoena through the RCMP, my options were limited in dealing with the situation.

At this point, after holding onto my pain for all those years, I was left with my final option. There was literally nothing I could do, other than to forgive the person. **To forgive.**

This was asking something of me that was impossible, in my eyes. I had held on to the hurt and pain and bitterness for so long, but I knew deep down that it was never going to get me anywhere. I was tired and weary of holding on to the pain. I wanted to be healed of the hurt.

> **Then Peter came to him and asked, "Lord, how often should I forgive someone who sins against me? Seven times?" "No, not seven times,"
> Jesus replied, "but seventy times seven!"**
> (Matthew 18:21-22)

The point of that conversation was not necessarily to give a numerical answer of four hundred and ninety times we should forgive, but to illustrate that it is ongoing.

Some days, I truly felt this. I could say to this person "I forgive you and what you did to me", other days, it was harder. It was like I had to forgive this person every day, over and over again. If I were to take the number literally, over the course of seven + years, if I forgave the person every single day, we'd be looking at over 2500 times.

If I left it at 490 times, and decided to stop forgiving then, I would go right back to feeling angry, sad, bitter. I do feel those emotions on some days still, but the only person still hurting then is ME.

Forgiving this person is still something I am working on doing, continually. Forgiveness is not easy. You need to do it over and over and over again.

That was when I began to realize that it wasn't my place to play judge towards this person. If I wanted to let go of the pain, I had to trust that God would take it from me, and that He would deal with it, Himself.

After not dealing with the trauma of this event in a very unhealthy way, I also deeply needed forgiveness for things I had done. In my pain, I caused others deep pain.

If you forgive those who sin against you, your heavenly Father will forgive you. But if you refuse to forgive others, your Father will not forgive your sins.
(Matthew 6:14-15)

I am not going to pretend I am a total rock star at forgiveness now. I'm not. But I did pray for this person, and while I struggled to not let bitterness back into my soul, over time, I found my prayer went from something like:

"Dear Jesus, please let him know how much he has screwed up my life, and possibly smite him, if you haven't already."

To a prayer something a little more like:

"Dear Jesus, please help me to forgive him. Please let the bitterness and hate I feel towards him disappear, and please heal him."

My thoughts of him turned from hate to thoughts of compassion. I don't know what the statistics are, but I do know that someone who has been sexually abused as a child can go one of two directions.

I am not overlooking or justifying his actions, but there are things that happen to people that really mess them up. Hurt people hurt people. It takes a chain breaker to overcome that.

Forgiving someone for doing something horrible to another person is not an easy thing. But when we are warned about the seriousness of not forgiving, I deeply knew I needed to forgive to move on from the fear and anxiety that was literally crippling me. I had done wrong too. I needed to break an unbreakable chain.

Just as God forgave me, I had to let go of those chains that were holding my life back- all of the chains. I had to let it go and truly forgive people who had hurt me. To forgive someone is to release the chains you are holding onto, and to release myself from the burden that I did not have to carry.

"Lord, help!" they cried in their trouble, and He saved them from their distress. He led them from the darkness and deepest gloom; He snapped their chains. Let them

praise the Lord for His great love and for the wonderful
things he has done for them. For He broke down their
prison gates of bronze; He cut apart their bars of iron.
(Psalm 107:13-16)

He sets us free! I had to forgive, and place my pain into God's
hands. It would consume me otherwise.

When I am afraid, I put my trust in you. In God, whose
word I praise, in God I trust; I shall not be afraid.
What can flesh do to me?
(Psalm 56:3-4)

If I can trust that God forgave me for everything I had done in
my own life, I could trust God to take the pain and hurts I've
experienced in life, and release me from the grief and fear and
bitterness of un-forgiveness.

God will judge; that's not my job. I did not have to keep holding
onto my insatiable need to seek justice or revenge or whatever
I happened to be feeling.

I could not make sense of a lot of situations in life, because
there doesn't seem to have any sense to it.

Commit everything you do to the Lord. Trust Him, and
He will help you. He will make your innocence radiate
like the dawn, and the justice of your cause will shine
like the noonday sun. Be still in the presence of the
Lord, and wait patiently for Him to act. Don't worry
about evil people who prosper or fret about their wicked
schemes. Stop being angry! Turn from your rage!
Do not lose your temper- it only leads to harm.
For the wicked will be destroyed, but those who
trust in the Lord will possess the land forever.
(Psalm 37:5-8)

We are all so broken. We will never understand exactly why certain situations happen. But maybe it is not our place to know. However, it is my place to move on; to forgive and to choose love instead of hate.

Turn away from evil and do good. Search for peace, and work to maintain it.
(Psalm 34:14)

Forgiveness does not mean that you are initiating a relationship with a perpetrator. Forgiveness isn't because they are deserving of being forgiven either, just as we aren't deserving of forgiveness from God.

Forgiveness is a gift, and a choice from within us. Forgiving has nothing to do with someone being sorry. It is often very one sided, in fact.

Forgive is a verb, therefore, an action word. It's an action that *you* need to do. Nowhere does it mention what the other person needs to do to receive forgiveness- they may never seek your forgiveness.

It's about *you* deciding to forgive them, regardless if they are sorry or not. The funny thing about forgiveness being *my choice* is that I am also the one who benefits.

In my case, the person may never even know I've forgiven them. I don't need to search them out to let him know I've forgiven them. We don't always have that opportunity in life. Forgiveness is as much for my own good as it is for the person who hurt me, if not more.

If a person is not sorry for what they have done, don't keep yourself in a position where they can continue to hurt you, but instead, do something Jesus does for us, even if this doesn't make any sense. **Just love them.**

> **"But for those who are willing to listen, I say, love your enemies! Do good to those who hate you. Bless those who curse you. Pray for those who hurt you... Love your enemies. Do good to them. Lend to them without expecting to be repaid. Then your reward in heaven will be very great and you will truly be acting as children of the Most High, for He is kind to those who are unthankful and wicked. You must be compassionate, just as your Father is compassionate. Do not judge others, and you will not be judged. Do not condemn others, and it will not come back against you. Forgive others and you will be forgiven."**
> (Luke 6:27-28; 35-37)

As I struggled to forgive people who have hurt me, I slowly began to understand how hard must it have been for Jesus to come to die on a cross to forgive the world of its sins?

If it was always so hard for me to forgive, why would I figure it would be easy for Jesus to forgive me? Going through the process of forgiving, I began to understand the heart of God.

I could keep focusing on the bad things in my life, or I could use those less-than-ideal events to learn from and to make me a better person, trying to be how Jesus wants me to be- more like Him.

It is always our own choice on how we react to the circumstances of life, but just as I had done things I am not proud of while trying to drink my pain away, I knew if I wanted to be forgiven, I needed to also forgive.

Work at living in peace with everyone, and work at living a holy [set apart] life, for those who are not holy [set apart] will not see the Lord. Look after each other so that none of you fails to receive the grace of God. Watch out that no poisonous roots of bitterness grows up to trouble you, corrupting many.

You have come to Jesus, the one who mediates a new covenant between God and people, and to the sprinkled blood, which speaks of forgiveness instead of crying out for vengeance like the blood of Abel. Be careful you do not refuse to listen to the One who is speaking.
(Hebrews 12:14-15; 24-25)

Holding onto pain and unforgiveness only denies yourself the gift of grace we all hope we receive when we mess up. And that's exactly what Jesus did when He went to the cross, so He could conquer death- our idea of death and the actual proof that we have a living God. He controls even death, and with that, life as well.

And then he invites us to join Him in His kingdom- Heaven. If that's not amazing grace, I don't know what is. He forgave us, so let's not hold forgiveness back from anyone. Even if we think they don't deserve it. They probably and most certainly don't. But then again, do we?

Someone once told me that grace isn't black and white. It's a shade of grey. And that was the most gracious thing to say, especially because it was said to me. I was feeling unworthy. But He knows my heart. He knows all of our hearts- our intentions, our thoughts, our actions.

That's why we need to keep ourselves completely out of the judgement process. That is for God and God alone. He knows the full picture. We do not.

We are confident of all this because of our great trust in God through Christ. It is not that we think we are qualified to do anything on our own. Our qualification comes from God. He has enabled us to be ministers of the new covenant. This is a covenant not of written laws, but of the Spirit. The old written covenant ends in death, but under the new covenant, the Spirit gives life.
(2 Corinthians 3:4-6)

Redeeming Coupons

As I began reading my Bible more and more, a word that I had struggled with was **redemption**. It was repeated so many times throughout the Bible, and it was also a word that was used regularly in church, but it was such a hard word for me to grasp its meaning. A lot of things that church people say are confusing.

"Redemption" is not really a word that comes up in most conversations, so I made a point of continuing to not use the word. I like to use normal words to explain, personally.

Just like Harry and Lloyd, the idea of redemption is coming back from a terrible decision.

> **"...you go and do something like this...
> And totally redeem yourself!"**

Even though I grew up at church, some of the words weren't ever really explained, so I just went with it, and didn't use the words I didn't know how to explain. But in reality, words explain at lot and words are actually packed with a lot of meaning.

As much as I tried to ignore it, it was a word that continued to ring in my brain, so I started to look into its meaning. Instead of ignoring it because it was a difficult concept, much like the concept of love, it is a theme strewn across the Bible, so it must be important.

The more I looked into the word, the more I became curious about the meaning, and how to wrap my brain around not just the word, but the application of it to my own life.

I asked my friends to help understand it, and thought of instances in everyday life where we would use the idea of redeeming. We redeem coupons, gift cards, funds.

The Google definitions of redemption also helped make the concept a little clearer.

Redemption *(noun)*

1. The action of saving or being saved from sin, error or evil.

Syn. Saving, freeing from sin, absolution

2. The action of regaining or gaining possession of something in exchange for payment, or clearing a debt.

Syn. Retrieval, recovery, reclamation, repossession, return

Which led me to the word, absolution.

Absolution *(noun)*

1. Formal release from guilt, obligation or punishment.

Syn. Forgiveness, pardon, exoneration, remission, dispensation, indulgence, clemency, mercy.

Those definitions began to paint a picture in my mind. Not of redeeming coupons, but of how the word applies to my life.

Redemption. Sacrifice. Ransomed. Reconciliation. Rescued. Forgiven.

As I was beginning to wrap my mind around what it meant to be redeemed, I came across so many points in the Bible where it talked about redemption as means of adopting us into God's family. This is what God truly wants for us, as His children, and our relationship with Him takes on a whole different look.

**In love, he predestined us for adoption as sons through
Jesus Christ, according to the purpose of his will.**
(Ephesians 1:5)

Adoption is close to home in my family. It is something I can relate to. My beautiful sister is adopted. When my parents adopted my sister, they *wanted* her as a part of our family, including her as a daughter. She was chosen to be a part of our family. It's a beautiful picture of how God wants us to be a family.

God wants us in *His* family. He chose us. And He wants us to choose to be in His family. We are not meant to be slaves. God has made us His family, heirs to His throne. It doesn't get more personal than that. Knowing God like this puts an entirely different picture into my mind. He created us to love us.

I could live with this idea of being accepted as a child of God, but with that does come more difficult aspects of having a relationship with God; nowhere does it ever say that life will be easy. Why can't it be easy?

The idea of redemption is so much deeper than being adopted. There is so much more to it. The reality of adoption is complicated, somewhat painful, for all parties involved. Like an onion, so many layers.

**For all who are led by the Spirit of God are children
of God. So you have not received a spirit that
makes you fearful slaves. Instead, you received
God's Spirit when he adopted you as His own
children. Now we call Him, "Abba, Father."**

**For His Spirit joins with our spirit to affirm that we
are God's children, we are His heirs. In fact, together**

**with Christ, we are heirs of God's glory. But if we
share His glory, we must also share His suffering.**
(Romans 8:14-17)

We were heirs to Him. If we agree to it, we become His children,
an heir; children who would receive an inheritance. But the
idea of being an heir also requires a death before receiving an
inheritance. The idea of a will or a covenant is a legal contract
that requires a guarantee; it's a promise, a commitment.

**But when the right time came, God sent His Son, born
of a woman, subject to the law. God sent him to buy
freedom for us who were slaves to the law, so that He
could adopt us as His very own children. And because
we are His children, God has sent the Spirit of his Son
into our hearts prompting us to call out, "Abba, Father."
Now you are no longer a slave but God's own child. And
since you are His child, God has made you His heir.**
(Galatians 4:4-7)

He didn't create us so that he could strike us down with
lightning every time we messed up. God doesn't want us to
view him as some sort of God with a beard and spear like Zeus
up in heaven; unreachable. He didn't create us to live a life that
wasn't worth living. God wants us to have a very personal
relationship with Him- to be family.

Why the need for a sacrifice at all? Can't we simply just be
friends? It confused me for a long time about why Jesus even
needed to die in this plan. God was not only wanting us as His
own children. He also wanted us to live a free life.

However, we were not only like orphans, we were actually
worse off than that. We were essentially slaves to the rules of
life and death. Even though we were considered slaves, He

never treated us like slaves, but as deeply loved family. But slaves need to be bought at a price; a heavy cost.

God's will and original covenant was not fulfilled contractually, not because of God's part, but because of the people included in the covenant- they had to keep their part of the contract by following the rules. And they couldn't do it.

Thus the need for a new covenant, where Jesus's death and sacrifice was ultimately required. Jesus came to the world, to replace the first covenant with the second, a perfect covenant; God's promise to us. God knew that our sacrifices would never be enough. No amount of money could redeem us.

This is why He is the one who mediates a new covenant between God and people, so that all who are called can receive an eternal inheritance God has promised them. For Christ died to set them free from under the penalty of the sins they had committed under that first covenant. Now when someone leaves a will, it is necessary to prove that the person who made it is dead. The will only goes into effect after the person's death. While the person who made it is still alive, the will cannot be put into effect. This is why even the first covenant was put into effect with the blood of an animal... (22) In fact, according to the Law of Moses, nearly everything was purified with blood. For without the shedding of blood, there is no forgiveness.
(Hebrews 9:15-19; 22)

God was graciously taking out the possibility of failure for us. Now, it became a much different process. We can't earn God's love, and the only way we will ever be able to receive the promise of our inheritance is through the death of Jesus, who did just that to prove His love to us.

God's entire plan for the world, for our lives, was to live in peace and harmony with each other. God's will and purpose for us could not come to be until blood was shed for us, He had to die to fulfill His own will.

The question is not if it actually happened; history books tell us that Jesus was a real person; that this really happened- he was crucified. The question is, do you believe that Jesus was who he said he was? Do you believe that he is the Son of God, who came to save the world and bring us life, and life after death?

> **Through Christ you have come to <u>trust in God</u>. And you placed your faith and hope in God because he raised Christ from the dead and gave him great glory. You were cleansed from your sins when you obeyed the truth, so now you must show sincere love to each other as brothers and sisters. Love each other deeply with all your heart. For you have been born again, but not to a life that will quickly end. Your new life will last forever because it comes from the eternal, living word of God.**
> (1 Peter 1:21-23)

Jesus's life was a sacrifice, a ransom for mine, even when I didn't deserve it. None of us deserve it. World religions are completely contrary to Jesus; the need to admit that we will never be deserving of salvation is not an easy admission. It's surrendering our desire to deserve salvation.

Acknowledging that we are wrong is never easy. I think that's what turns a lot of people off of God- admitting that we can't do it without Him, which is ultimately giving up the idea that "we are god". We like to think that we can be good enough to get to heaven; we aren't as bad as the next person; we can do it ourselves. We are the center of our own worlds, until we can admit that we aren't.

He became the ransom for my life; He is someone who never did anything wrong in his entire life. We could **never** be enough for God. Not without Jesus.

> **For you know that God paid a ransom to save you from the empty life you inherited from your ancestors. And it was not paid with mere gold and silver, which lose their value. It was the precious blood of Christ, the sinless, spotless Lamb of God. God chose Him as your ransom long before the world began, but now in these last days he has been revealed for your sake.**
> (1 Peter 1:18-20)

But God wanted us, still. Because we were all given free will, angels included, we are in such a complicated war that it couldn't be as simple as using money. It is literally a war of eternal death and life. It had to be a war won with blood, not money to ransom us. Because, ironically, like the credit card slogan, "There are some things money can't buy."

YOU ARE PRICELESS.

I believe that we were created by God, and the world was created perfectly. I also believe that life is not how we were meant to be living as it stands now. Earth and life came to be, somehow, and while I am not a scientist, I am a designer, and I truly believe we were created by God; I can see it in the impossible details.

There is so much planning that goes into something as simple as a house, that I cannot believe that there was not an Ultimate

Plan and a Planner behind something as complicated as the universe and everything in it.

Adam and Eve were tempted by Satan with the idea that they could have as much knowledge as God. They wanted to be their own god. They wanted to see the whole picture. And that disobedience and desire was the downfall of civilization as we know it. That is when death and pain entered the perfect world God had created.

God gave us choice and free will, and with that came good and bad. The whole reason we failed at the first covenant was because there was nothing that we could sacrifice to redeem ourselves for the original sin that we are all guilty of- not just Adam and Eve.

We would love to say we would never disobey God; they had just ONE rule God asked them not to break: don't eat the forbidden fruit. But what God was really asking of them was to make the choice to accept God for everything He is.

Our sentence for that sin is death. Our souls are being fought over, and Jesus's death was the ransom for our souls. The fight is between light and darkness; good and evil; heaven and hell.

So now there is no condemnation for those who belong to Christ Jesus. And because you belong to him, the power of the life-giving Spirit has freed you from the power of sin that leads to death.
(Romans 8:1-2)

Because Jesus died, and then came back to life after He was killed, this literally proved that He has power over death. Because He has that power, our lives can be saved from inevitable bodily death. But not spiritual death.

We were trapped as slaves to the dark side of this beautiful life. We are big fans of Star Wars in our family, but I feel a better movie analogy would be from Narnia, where Aslan had to lay down his life to appease the White Witch, even though Aslan's sacrifice of his own life was for the life of a traitor, regardless of being a child.

Like us, we were undeserving of a second chance, because we, as people, had already messed up the first covenant with God. God, being as faithful and true to His word as He is, regardless of our unfaithfulness, had incredible mercy and grace on us, and He again entered into a promise with us where our only requirement is to accept the "contract". Sign on the dotted line. And you are forever His. This could be comparable to a marriage certificate or an adoption certificate.

Yes, Adam's one sin brings condemnation for everyone, but Christ's one act of righteousness brings a right relationship with God, and new life for everyone.
(Romans 5:18)

We just need to believe that God's sacrifice was **all** we need. Love is all you need, and God is that love.

I think that generally, people like to believe in heaven or life after death, but the majority of world religions require you to work at it, as to deserve salvation. In my mind, I think the biggest difference between world religions and of following Jesus is the lack of needing to work up different levels to salvation. Religion generally has a set of rules for one to follow and when you follow them all, you become a good person and you deserve that salvation all because YOU did it.

But with following Jesus, we are accepting that we have salvation and eternal life, not because we did it, but because

Jesus did what He did for us. He redeemed us when we didn't deserve it, but He did it because He made us; we were his masterpieces, and He sees us as PRICELESS!

"Because you are precious in my eyes, and honoured, and I love you, I give men in return for you, peoples in exchange for your life." Fear not, I am with you; I will bring your offspring from the east, and from the west, I will gather you. I say to the north, Give up, and to the south, Do not withhold; bring my sons from afar and my daughters from the end of the earth, everyone who is called by my name, whom I created for my glory, whom I formed and made"
(Isaiah 43:4-7)

Wow. I had always wanted to feel like I was precious in someone's eyes. And I began to realize that I was. I was this whole time. Even though I didn't always understand it, and I didn't feel it, I was precious. I was a prized possession of God.

But to accept that my life's ransom was someone else's life was still not something I felt deserving of. That should break anyone's heart. How is my life worth more than anyone else's?

I've never been in a hostage situation, but I can imagine it would feel something like the hopelessness of how my life felt. Utter despair, being completely alone, ready to give up. I can imagine, after being trapped for years, how good it would feel to be released from chains, only to realize that someone had to die so that I could be free.

Our ransom was not just a government payout. We were captured by an enemy; if you believe in good, then you have to believe in bad. Our lives were bought back from the dark lives we could have been slaves to for the rest of our existence.

Why should he die for me, someone so broken and imperfect? He died a horrific death for me on a cross. He died for you, for me, for us all.

> **For there is one God, and there is one mediator between God and man, Christ Jesus, who gave himself as a <u>ransom for all</u>, which is the testimony given at the proper time.**
> (1 Timothy 2: 5-6)

Having been so close to choosing death at points in my life, because of how desperately broken I was, I understand that death is the ultimate consequence of sin. I was so broken and fallen that I truly wanted to die.

My life was not right at all. I likely would have died had God not been with me through those years. Satan wants us to live a life like that. But that was not the life God wants for me or for anyone to live.

He ransomed me out of a life where I was broken, a slave to addiction and turmoil; he rescued me from what I could have become. He took me out of my misery, and changed my life to the point that I was unrecognizable to my own self.

> **For God was in Christ, reconciling the world to Himself, no longer counting people's sins against them. And He gave us this wonderful message of reconciliation. So we are Christ's ambassadors; God is making His appeal through us. We speak for Christ when we plead,**
> **"Come back to God!"**
> (2 Corinthians 5:19-20)

As hard as it has been for me to accept it, and really understand it, I believe it. So then, I will live for Him. Because of God sacrificing his Son, Jesus, I can finally live; and so I can have a life worth living. For everything that I had done in my life that was less than lovely; for all the hurt I had caused to myself, to others, to God; I am loved regardless.

Regardless of how undeserving I am, I am so loved. Regardless love.

Hope

What shall we say about such wonderful things as these? If God is for us, who can ever be against us? Since He did not spare even His own Son but gave Him up for us all, won't He also give us everything else?
(Romans 8:31-32)

Love found me. The moment I began understanding love, pure love, I began understanding life. I needed to accept love and to love myself in order to love another.

Purpose brought me understanding of pure love, and in understanding that love, I found purpose. My purpose is life. My purpose is love. The words come back to my mind. Love will live. Those words uttered to me in a coffee shop.

When I began to see how it was to love someone as a parent, it helped me make sense of how God saw me. In the simplest of explanations, for me, creating a life created some purpose for me.

As I continued learning about my relationship with God, and how He saw me, I began to discover a basic purpose of life. Once I had found some purpose in my life, I felt incredibly grateful to have made it to that point. It's a point of no return, really. It was a new chapter in my life. I had something to live for. I had some hope.

I felt like I had spent a lot of time in my life looking for my purpose; I probably could have done more praying about it, but God blessed me with a really beautiful life with my family. He gave me a future and a hope, even though I didn't begin looking for Him with my whole heart until after realizing how much He gave me.

Basic biology confirms a sense of purpose. Why are we here on earth? In the most uncomplicated sense, species are here to reproduce. I always knew that was part of the purpose of life, on the grand scheme of things, but I had to actually experience it before my mind understood. It was a humbling thing, to find out that this was part of my purpose.

Yet, my purpose was actually not about me, and my entire life had been entirely about myself up until this point. I had spent a huge period of my life, on my own and through therapy, thinking about what my purpose could possibly be, and what it meant to be happy and satisfied with my life.

Had I not gotten pregnant and had my son, I might still be searching for purpose. Or maybe I simply began to realize that life had become part of my purpose.

But there was still something more. Not everyone has children, and that certainly doesn't mean that their life is purposeless. I know we can have many purposes throughout our lives. It was difficult enough just finding one purpose, but we are here on this world for more than just reproducing. We are not limited to a basic biological purpose.

I am a mom, a woman, a daughter, etc. Those are all titles I have, and those are definitely part of who I am- part of the reason why I am alive.

But at the very root of it, I am a creation who is so loved. I am created and chosen by God to be in existence. That is who I am. But I had to find the purpose in the pain.

God knows the plans He has for our lives, but we are told we need to seek it out. Complacency and searching in the wrong places are why people search and some never get to find their true purpose, whether they give up trying to find it or they never got the chance to find it.

I do, however, believe that everyone needs to define for themselves what their own purpose is. That's the beauty of free will.

If you aren't doing what you are meant to do with your life, why aren't you? There is a huge underlying fear of failure that keeps people from being successful in life.

This is where it gets real. Just like our basic needs, Food, Shelter and Community, we also have that when it comes to who we really are and what we are meant to be in life: Physical, Mental, and Spiritual. Again, picture a nice triangle. With a little input from my design background here, but things just work best when there are three.

Essentially, we are a species; a creation consisting of those three aspects- Physical, Mental, and Spiritual. Again, we cannot survive without that little triangle that makes us whole. Without accepting that we need all three aspects to really be whole, we are going to struggle throughout life until death.

Just as we have a physical purpose, we also have a mental purpose. A huge element that held me back mentally was my anxiety. I suffered for a lot of years without knowing how to deal with it. It is still something that I suffer with, but have now learned many ways to deal with it.

I started creating lists (and lists) of goals when I was young. My dad sat me down one day, and told me to write out a list of what my goals in life where. I did it, but had no idea why he wanted me to do this.

Years later I found one of my goal lists, and was shocked at how many things I had done off the list. It wasn't like I was holding onto the list, either. I had to dust it off to read the writing. But somehow, those goals, written years previously, became the subconscious bucket list for my life.

College, check.
Travel, check.
See Jack Johnson in concert, check.
Whitewater Rafting, check.
Summit a Mountain, check.
Have kids, double check.
Write a book. You get it.

At the time, I didn't understand the importance of having goals. It gives you purpose. It gives you drive. You can accomplish a lot when you *want* to do something; when you are passionate about something.

I struggled for a long time about not knowing my purpose in life. That being said, I know my life had purpose, before my son and even despite my son, whether I knew it or not. Looking back on life always gives you 20/20 vision; all the struggles I had been through somehow grew me into a stronger person.

Each experience I have had in my life is unique to me, and whether I like it or not, it's turned me into the person I am; the purpose of my life is revealed throughout those experiences.

I may not be able to bench press much, but I now feel like a really strong person, with purpose; always growing, learning, experiencing. And we are not limited to a single purpose in life.

Having goals in life is part of finding the purpose of life. Not everyone's purpose is the same. I can't spell it out for any other person. What my goals are in life are not going to be the same goals as everyone else in the world. If everyone's goals were the same, I'd be signing up for the next sky-diving flight. It's just not going to happen.

Remember the movie, The Bucket List? Well, isn't that how we should live every day of our lives? Like it was our last? But I don't think we should be rushed about needing to fit in all those things we wished we had done in our lives.

That's the exciting thing about life. You never know where life will take you and which box is going to get crossed off next. But having a plan and goals to work towards is most certainly a starting place.

There is something incredibly rewarding about crossing things off the "to-do" list. You experience feelings of accomplishment and pride. As my son would say, "I do-ed it!!"

On one of my later, more evolved goal list, I started breaking down my goals into categorical listing, because I am a little bit dorky like that. Just do it! Write it down.

Personal Goals.
(ex. Start a garden; learn German)

Physical Goals.
(ex. Run a half marathon; take dance lessons)

Financial Goals.
(ex. Buy a house; put $__/month into RRSPs)

Relationship/ Social Goals.
(ex. Meet a friend for coffee twice a week; have a date night)

Spiritual Goals.
(ex. Volunteer at an orphanage; join a study group)

I mentioned finding passion earlier. This is something a lot of people forget about. Part of finding your purpose lies in the question, what are you passionate about? What gets your blood boiling and/or lights up your face when the conversation comes up? Think about those things. Those things are inside of you for a reason.

Do what you love! We would lead a pretty unfulfilled life if we chose a career based on something we aren't passionate about. Maybe we chose the career because of the money or status that it gives us, but can we really thrive if we have chosen something we don't truly care about?

Instead of carrying on with the status quo, we can be very successful if we have passion in what we do and we can be content with our own achievements out of life. But more importantly than our own personal satisfaction, we are also to live as we are called.

As creations of God, we have been individually designed-uniquely and wonderfully. We have been given passions and purpose based on who we are, as individuals. We are all unique as humans; what one person is terrible at, another is brilliant at.

Only let each person lead a life that the Lord has assigned to him, and to which God has called him. That is my rule in all the churches.
(1 Corinthians 7:17)

But when you have a rule like that, what can really be holding you back? We can't force ourselves to be something that we are not.

**And we know that for those who love God all things
work together for good, for those who are called
according to His purpose.**
(Romans 8:28)

Did you see the catch? It will all work out... according to *His
purpose*. Not ours. We can try to do all this until we are blue in
the face. We can try on our own and search and search, and
all the while, His purpose for our lives and our idea of our
purpose for our lives may be not always be in harmony.

So now we need to worry about our own ideas of our purpose
and His purpose for our life. But we can believe in the promise
that it will be *good*. It may not be our own plans for our lives,
but it will be good.

**For I know the plans I have for you, declares the Lord,
plans for welfare and not for evil, to give you a future
and a hope. Then you will call upon me and come and
pray to me, and I will hear you. You will seek me and
find me, when you seek me with all your heart.**
(Jeremiah 29:11-13)

As we struggle to find out our physical purposes and our
mental purposes, if we are to neglect out spiritual purposes,
we will never be whole. That's where faith has to come in.

How can we know if our purpose for our life and God's
purpose for our lives are in line with each other?

I had grown up in a church family, went to the Christian
schools, Christian camps. I knew it all in my head. I had
countless verses memorized from the Bible, and I prayed, went
to church on and off throughout my early adult years. I used
to even travel an hour to get to church when I lived in Lake
Louise (not often, but I did it, sometimes).

Regardless of how far away I really was at points in my life from all of that, that spiritual element of my life is part of who I am. A big part. It took a lot for me to understand and process the complexity of faith.

In everything I had been through, I came to the realization that God had never given up on me, and never will. Even when I was giving up on myself, He was always there, quietly and patiently waiting for me to come back to Him.

He never left me. And He always quietly kept reminding me that He was there. Sometimes, when God is quiet, it is only because the noise around us is too loud, and you have to look back to realize the quiet whispering was, in fact, there.

"Be still and know that I am God! I will be honoured by every nation. I will be honoured throughout the world"
(Psalm 46:10)

I am so loved. And simply put, again, love is our purpose.

God wants us to accept that love; His love and His sacrifice was the ultimate purpose for the world. He sent His own Son, Jesus, to die for us to redeem us, and finally make sense of our mistruths about death. Death doesn't control our lives- only He does.

Now my soul is deeply troubled. Should I pray, 'Father, save me from this hour?' But this is the very reason I came!
(John 12:27)

Even Jesus was hurting, knowing His impending death and the consequent battle against the forces of death in those 3 days He was dead. And He did that because He loves us. Our spiritual, physical, and mental self is complete, in Jesus's love for us. We don't cease to exist when we die. That, my friend, is the art of living.

We need to have faith that this truly happened because of the fact that God loves us. We need to believe and accept that we are **SO LOVED**. We are created to have a purposefully fulfilled life.

That being said, I am convinced that the Bible and everything it is about can be summed up in two simple rules.

> **And he said to him, "You shall love the Lord your God with all your heart and with all your soul and with all your mind. This is the great and first commandment. And a second is like it: You shall love your neighbour as yourself."**
> (Matthew 22:37-40)

This is backed up many times throughout the Bible. These two, plain instructions.

Love your neighbour as yourself. It's just as equal the 'love your neighbours' part as it is the 'as yourself' part.

I have an easy time loving others. I am a pretty social being; I generally really like people.

Yet, I struggled so hard with loving myself. I didn't bring myself to love me for a long time. I never accepted that I was SO LOVED.

> **"You shall love your neighbor as yourself. Love does no wrong to a neighbor, therefore love is fulfilling of the law."**
> (Romans 13: 9-10)

It's not just a feeling. It's the law. It's God's simple, yet wildly difficult law. Yet, love is a choice. You can choose to break the law or not. It is your choice. It's not always an easy choice, but you can accept it or not. You can share it with others, or not.

This is my new commandment, that you love others as I have loved you. Greater love has no one than this; that someone lay down his life for his friends. You are my friends if you do what I command you.
(John 15:12)

But don't be surprised when you suffer some consequences of breaking the law. Laws are meant to protect and guide so that everyone can have the best life possible.

As soon as someone thinks they are above the law, that's when people get hurt. Open your eyes!

God made a choice. And He chose me. And as broken as I am, God never said he couldn't use me. He said I was so loved.

I am loved because Jesus died on the cross to fulfill what the law legally required to have happen in order for me to be bought back at the highest cost, money can't even compare to this cost, so that I could receive my inheritance into God's family as a child of God.

Faith

Through all the struggles and figuring out what I really believed in, it all boiled down to this: with the experiences I've been through and the love I've felt, I can only equate it to my faith in God.

I don't have a glamourous argument here. I believe it because it feels right. I have been taught it, and I've lived it. I accept it with hope. Does it make sense? If you have faith, it does. But what's faith anyways? Faith is hope.

> **"For in hope we were saved. Now hope that is**
> **seen is not hope. For who hopes for what he sees?**
> **But if we hope for what we do not see, we**
> **wait for it with patience."**
> (Romans 8:24-25)

Faith is a complicated, yet simplistic aspect of life. How do I know what's real? I'm not sure what atheists think about this, but I think pretty much everyone in the world can accept that we are spiritual beings, on some level.

I can't explain it. I just know it. I feel it. That's faith. It's hope.

> **Therefore, since we have been made right in God's**
> **sight by faith, we have peace with God because of what**
> **Jesus Christ our Lord has done for us. Because of our**
> **faith, Christ brought us into this place of undeserved**
> **privilege where we now stand, and we confidently**
> **and joyfully look forward to sharing God's glory. We**
> **can rejoice too, when we run into problems and trials,**
> **for we know that they help us develop endurance.**

And endurance develops strength of character, and
character strengthens our confident hope of salvation.
And this hope will not lead to disappointment. For we
know how dearly God loves us, because He has given
us the Holy Spirit to fill our hearts with His love.
(Romans 5:1-5)

In my Bible, the title of that section is "Peace with God through
Faith" and it goes on to talk about all this suffering. While
peace and suffering don't seem to go hand in hand, after
experiencing the suffering aspect of it, and coming to peace
with it, faith has become so real to me! It's the mystery of faith;
it is beyond comprehension and explanation. It literally is a
leap of faith.

SUFFERING
ENDURANCE
CHARACTER
HOPE.
(Romans 5:3-4)

When I think of all this, I fall to my knees and pray
to the Father, the Creator of everything in heaven and
on earth. I pray that from His glorious, unlimited
resources He will empower you with inner strength
through His Spirit. Then Christ will make His home
in your hearts as you trust in Him. Your roots will
grow down into God's love and keep you strong.

And may you have the power to understand, as all God's
people should, how wide, how long, how high and how
deep His love is. May you experience the love of Christ,
though it is too great to understand fully. Then you
will be made complete with all the fullness of life and
power that comes from God. Now all glory to God, who

is able, through His mighty power at work within us, to accomplish infinitely more than we might ask or think.
(Ephesians 3:14-20)

For years, I relied on myself, and found myself wondering if God really had my best interests. I found myself questioning time and time again, why He would allow bad things to happen, and if He really loved me. Hindsight is 20/20, and it often revealed to me much later that everything happens for a reason.

Sometimes pieces fall together in your mind in certain seasons, whether they are seasons of loneliness or terrible grief. Part of hindsight is the reflection of the circumstance, rather than burying the pain. Address it, acknowledge it. And don't try to do it alone. There are so many resources out there to help heal.

Looking back allows the lessons to be learned. What could have been done differently? What was in my control? What wasn't in my control? If the situation came up again, how could I deal with it the next time? Suffering really does build endurance.

It often took so much more time to heal that I expected, but there was always a reason, for every single thing that I counted as bad. Out of the bad, came healing, not just for myself, but others with me.

Through sharing my own experiences with my friends, I often saw some healing in their lives. Had I not gone through those difficult circumstances and really experienced the pain, how could I relate to their pain?

Together, we were able to heal. It certainly wasn't something I would wish on anyone, but looking back, given the choice, I don't think I would change any part of my life. That is coming to peace with life through hope that there is something to be learned out of the situation.

Moving forward throughout life, I know there will be hard, heart-breaking elements, but having the faith that there is a reason for it has made facing challenges an easier task. And looking forward to life past this life on earth puts the "everyday challenges" into a new perspective.

> **My heart has heard you say, "Come and talk with me." And my heart responds, "Lord I'm coming."**
> (Psalm 27:8)

One day, I was struggling with my anxiety: my oldest was just out of school, the youngest was waking up every two hours, and the daily grind at this point just felt hard.

I was trying to take out my frustrations and anxiety on the kitchen and bathrooms, and while panic cleaning, furiously scrubbing the toilet, something pricked my conscience. *"Be like Mary"*.

Even though I was busy doing mom things, I knew it wasn't a reference to Mary, the mother of Jesus. No, it was a friend of Jesus', who couldn't put down her toilet scrubbing while Jesus was at their house, chatting, and enjoying each other's company.

> **But the Lord answered her, "Martha, Martha, you are anxious and troubled about many things, there is only one thing worth being concerned about. Mary has discovered it, and it will not be taken away from her."**
> (Luke 10:41 (NKJ); 42 (ESV))

While I was anxiously busy scrubbing and cooking and changing diapers, had I taken a moment to set down everything, and listen to Jesus? Had I taken a moment to focus on Jesus and be thankful for everything I have; everything that God has given to me in my life?

That one and only thing is Jesus. Instead of being worried about all the little things that life throws our direction, we are to focus only on him, as Mary did. Not distracted like Martha. I needed to be sitting down, focusing on and listening to what Jesus had to say. And only that.

> **Purify me from my sins, and I will be clean; wash me and I will be whiter than snow. Oh, give me my joy back again; you have broken me- now let me rejoice. Don't keep looking at my sins. Remove the stain of my guilt. Create a loyal spirit within me.**
> (Psalm 51:7-11)

No amount of scrubbing yourself can clean your life up to the point it needs to be. This is why we need to look to Jesus. Ironically, that thought came to me after I felt a prodding to clean my house.

Listen when you feel that prodding. Send that text to your friend. Bring over a little gift for a friend. You don't know the waterfall effect that could have on someone's life. You don't get to see the whole picture. That's the beauty of trusting that God's got the whole picture. That's living with faith in action.

> **If then you have been raised with Christ, seek things that are above, where Christ is, seated at the right hand of God. Set your minds on things that are above, not on things that are on earth.**
> (Colossians 3:2)

Good Father

God is a good Father. I know that not everyone has a good father, but God is a good Father. Everything is in His plan, regardless of how much it doesn't make sense to us; no matter how deeply it hurts us.

But sometimes, the things that God decides to allow are part of a beautiful picture we just aren't able to see until we look back and see the picture in its fullness; its intricacy; its complexity.

We are shown only a portion of His beautiful artwork, His masterplan. Who are we to question?

Over the years, I would be shown again and again that there is always a reason for everything that happens. But sometimes, what the reason is, I may never know why God puts us back into a season of life I thought I was out of.

> **"For everything there is a season, and a time for every matter under heaven, a time to be born and a time to die, a time to plant and a time to pluck up what is planted, a time to weep and a time to laugh, a time to mourn and a time to dance, a time to love and a time to hate, a time for war and a time for peace."**
> (Ecclesiastes 3:1-2, 4 and 8)

Maybe the lessons I had learned in my younger years were being forgotten, or I was becoming complacent in life; perhaps it was to finally connect the dots in these lessons I had to learn over and over. Whatever the reason, I was placed back into a familiar season; one that I didn't want to be in.

As I had learned with God, whatever the lesson, He would carry me through. His lessons are always to reflect His love for us and through us.

October 15, 2016 was strangely similar to the exact day the year before. I had a hair appointment that day, and I remember thinking, 'Wow, I had a hair appointment today, exactly one year ago last year.'

I do not have an overly impressive memory, nor do I have a scheduled life.

The only reason I remembered that I had a hair appointment, was because I never actually got a haircut that day. As I was waiting in the lobby to get my hair cut at of my favourite hair salon, I got a phone call being informed that my son's arm was likely broken.

I had rushed from my hair appointment up to the hospital, to see my sweet son in pain, with a broken elbow. I had felt so bad that I wasn't there for my son in the moment of his accident, but his daddy was there. He was being a good daddy.

Over the years, I've pictured him carefully placing our son into his car seat, or more likely just in the front seat of his truck, because I imagine it had terrified him to move our son's broken arm.

I may not know the logistics of how he got our son into the car, but I do know he did it with so much love. I heard the fear in his voice when he called me. It was that sound where immediately you knew something was wrong. But I knew he had it under control.

After a sleepless night, we got sent to a hospital 2.5 hours away for surgery. We cried together as we drove our little boy to the hospital. It broke my heart to see him in pain, and I could do nothing about it for him. All I could do was whisper to him, 'it will be okay, it will be okay.'

Deep down, I knew it would be okay, but it still broke my heart in the moment. Time heals broken bones. But there was nothing I could do other than to comfort my son in his pain.

~

Fast forward exactly one year to the day.

My son's arm had completely healed, but this is why I had my flashback, as I had coincidentally booked a hair appointment on that exact day, exactly one year later. October 15. I clearly remember feeling a sense of relief that my son was with me today, a year later.

While I can't control accidents, I still wanted to. At this point in life, I was running a day home, and accident prevention was a pretty serious source of anxiety in my life. It was an accident, and besides bubble wrapping children, nothing could have prevented it.

On our way back to the house, I had to fill up with gas, and that's when I heard ambulances heading out. Sirens had always given me an uneasy feeling, yet this time, a sense of fear really hit me.

I immediately felt a lump in my throat, said a prayer, and hoped everything would be okay with whatever the situation was that the first responders were heading out to.

I felt tears coming to my eyes, so I hugged my boy, while he was seated in his car seat, and continued back home.

Later that afternoon, I saw an article online that, in my mind, was one of the worst things that can happen in life. It was an article that confirmed that a toddler had been killed in a vehicle accident.

I knew it was the sirens that I had heard earlier. My heart absolutely broke for the family of this child. I didn't know who it was, but from the description of the situation, I felt that it was no one I possibly could know, despite the small town we live in.

Still, I was devastated at the thought of someone losing their child. That is the worst thing a parent can ever experience. It's unimaginable loss.

A few of the day home providers discussed it, all of us praying that it was not one of the kids we took care of. You truly love those little kiddos you care for.

That night, a close friend asked to come over, and although it was quite late, I figured she needed to talk about something important, and I was ready to listen. But the second she walked through our door, I knew something was very wrong. I didn't realize the conversation was going to be related to those sirens.

It was Uta, one of the beautiful children that I took care of.

I was so beyond shocked. I had even checked in with all the day home parents that lived in the area where the accident was reported to have happened. In all honesty, she had never even crossed my mind, as that was not the area of town she lived in. This was not even a possibility in my mind.

The despair I felt truly brought me to my knees. My friend held me as I wept on the stairs, and we sat, feeling so broken together.

It was the gut wrenching sadness, the agony of my heart literally breaking. It was the pain I knew all too well.

I couldn't believe it was her. Sweet little Uta. My heart was shattered. This family had something very special about them. They loved their daughter with all their heart; she was their world. She was so loved. It was truly evident.

I couldn't comprehend why God takes children away. I don't pretend to understand it. It is a very unnatural thing for children to die before their parents. That's not how life is ever supposed to turn out.

There truly are no words. Tears say enough.

I didn't know why God allowed this to happen, yet again. What I do know is that God made himself incredibly known to me over the next months, and very much so the next days after the tragedy, and I also knew that God can make anything beautiful, even the most devastating circumstances.

With tears endlessly flowing, I had prayed the night I found out about Uta's death that God would be able to use me in whatever way He could.

I prayed to see some hope in the situation. I felt like I was asking Him the impossible. How could there be any hope in something like this?

"Likewise the Spirit helps us in our weakness. For we do not know what to pray for as we ought, but the Spirit himself intercedes for us with the groanings too deep for words."
(Romans 8:26)

The day after the accident, I felt the overwhelming need to go to my church, like I was being drawn there, feeling very hopeless for the situation, but I knew I was being drawn there.

I didn't sleep that night, and the next morning, I went alone to church. That was the only place I wanted to be. I felt so broken again, but not like the times before.

It was a bigger pain; a grieving parent's pain. A pain that was so much bigger than me. A pain that was completely out of my control.

I walked in and was immediately greeted with a hug rather than the typical handshake from one of the ladies I didn't know well. She just looked at me, and drew me into her arms.

Even though she didn't know what was going on, I think she could sense my deep grief, and her compassionate gesture was exactly what I needed at that moment. It would be a year later that I would learn that she had also lost a child, and in that moment, she was comforting me for the very thing she had suffered through.

I wept the entire service, and we prayed as a church, as a community for the family. In those moments, there was nothing that anyone can really say or do to make anything better. Praying for comfort for them was the only thing we could do at that point.

I was so overcome with grief. That afternoon, not knowing what else to do, I brought an orchid for them to their home. It was a gesture that in no way could ever be enough. That night, I cried with them on the phone. None of it was enough. It is so awful to not be able to do anything at all to take away their pain.

It was so hard to be in a place where you can't change what happened. All I wanted to do was take away their pain, give them their beautiful daughter back, or at the very least, say or do anything to make it better. But there are no words to fix it.

All I could do was offer them comfort, tea, whatever it was that they possibly needed.

However, God can use the impossible to prove what is truly possible. He can take a hopeless situation, regardless of how painful it is, and use it to show His unconditional love. Being so broken is exactly when God can show us how desperately we need Him.

I also know God had been preparing my heart for the majority of my life for this moment where I would find myself needing to comfort my dear friends' heart. I was ready now.

Most of my life I spent struggling with God and one of my biggest struggles was coming to terms with why Rachel, that beautiful seven year old had died. Perhaps it was because I knew the pain of losing a child, not in a personal, maternal sense, but I had struggled with processing Rachel's death since I was 11 years old.

**Who knows if perhaps you were made
queen for such a time as this?**
(Esther 4:14)

Time does not heal all wounds, but with the gift of time, I had also been able to see how life can still be beautiful, even after the death of a child. I knew the suffering in life was only for the time we are here.

Peace Heals Childhood Wounds

In the previous months, I had been suffering from a low grade migraine- one that was not bad enough to call in sick every day, but bad enough that I was having a hard time coping with it, and had a very foggy mind.

After the accident, I truly believe that God took that away from me so I could do whatever it was that needed to be done. God was comforting me, so that I could comfort my dear friends. It did not stop there. That was only the beginning.

I had booked a doctor appointment for my headaches before, but miraculously they had gone away by the time my appointment arrived. I still went to my appointment, despite the fact that 3 months of headaches had suddenly ended, which in my books are nothing short of a miracle. My broken heart and the anxiety I was suffering was my next cause for concern.

My doctor is an amazing doctor, and along with his family, I would consider them to be pretty close to being family. I am so thankful to have gotten to know them personally through my church.

Let me tell you, a broken heart actually hurts. I was broken hearted. I was devastated for the loss of life. My heart broke for my friend's loss of their daughter. I cried with my doctor, "Why can't there just be some happiness?"

To which he replied, "Maybe you are looking for the wrong thing; not happiness, **but peace.**"

He left me with not a prescription, but this from the Bible:

> **We are human, but we don't wage war as humans do.**
> **We use God's mighty weapons, to knock down the**
> **strongholds of human reasoning and to destroy false**
> **arguments. We destroy every proud obstacle that**
> **keeps people from knowing God. We capture their**
> **rebellious thoughts and teach them to obey Christ.**
> (2 Corinthians 10:3-5)

But we don't "wage war" like humans when we know God. We don't look at life the same way most people do. The war against death is over. He won.

> **The *wages* of sin is death, but the free gift of God**
> **is eternal life through Christ Jesus our Lord.**
> (Romans 6:23)

The cost of brokenness is death. But life is in Jesus, at His expense. He did what He did so that death would be defeated.

In the days and weeks after Uta's death, I felt like I was living in another world, another realm. My eyes were so open to so much more than my life, here on earth. It was as if the spiritual realm of my life crossed over into my daily reality, and I began to realize just how much more there had to be to life.

Throughout life, music has been a huge comfort. For years, I couldn't fall asleep without my iPod playing. I couldn't stand silence. During this time especially, I turned to music for comfort, back to the desperation for the silence to leave.

I found myself listening then to Chris Tomlin – Good Father, on repeat. All week.

> **Oh, it's love so undeniable I can hardly speak**
> **Peace so unexplainable I can hardly think**
> **As you call me deeper still into love**

Peace so unexplainable. It was the element that was missing in my life; the last piece to my life's puzzle. With as much turmoil that life had shown me, I had never been able to experience peace in life.

It began to make sense that there had to be more to life than our physical lives. If the desire of my heart is peace, I realized it could be only found in heaven if that's where my treasure is. To attain that treasure promised to me, meant I needed to experience death to my old ways.

I am given new life, beyond this physical life. We can experience peace, only through Jesus's gift of love.

Again, my eyes were opened to God's comfort and in the darkest moments, His love and light shone through.

You're a good, good Father, it's who you are
And I'm loved by you, it's who I am
Oh, and I've seen many searching for answers far and wide
But I know we're all searching for
answers only You provide
'Cause You know just what we need before we say a word

I had prayed for God to be able to use me and this situation for His glory, despite the hopelessness and pain of it all. I could have easily let myself become overwhelmed with grief, which I was at points, but not to the point of not being able to be useful.

Seeing the idea of eternity beyond life began to help me realize there is more to life than this. The irony is that it took this death to begin to understand life so much more.

God offered so much comfort to me that week, and I was able to let myself be used by God. I don't know how I was able to accomplish anything, other than knowing it was not myself, but God's strength and comfort that was helping me to push on.

I still could not understand why God would give and take away life like this. Losing a child this way was the worst thing that could possibly happen to anyone, ever. I think the world would agree.

How could a child's life be so valuable when it hurt so much having them taken away? How could her life be so valuable, if God could just take that life away so easily? Didn't He know how loved she was?

Didn't I know how loved I was as a child? I had listened to the lie and these "false arguments" that losing a child in this life was the worst possible thing to ever imagine. No! This was human reasoning that I had carried my whole life. It was the root of why I struggled accepting God's love as a child.

> **But Jesus said, "Let the little children come to me. Don't stop them! For the Kingdom of Heaven belongs to those who are like these children."**
> (Matthew 19:14)

As much as it hurts so deeply when we suffer a loss like this, I truly had peace with the fact that Uta was in heaven. She was in the most perfect place that this world cannot even offer. Everything earthly will eventually fade.

Children are so precious to God; to Jesus. Their innocent lives are so unaffected by the pain and horrors of the world. He wants to keep it that way for them. He wants to protect them, like a good Father wants to protect their child from harm.

**Store your treasure in heaven, where moth and
rust cannot destroy, and thieves do not break
in and steal. Wherever your treasure is, there
the desires of your heart will also be.**
(Matthew 6:20-21)

Our treasure is meant to be in heaven, not here on earth. Earth isn't the place it's meant to be, in the end. And children are a treasure to Jesus. Heaven is where He wants them! He wants His greatest treasure there. The worst possible things to now imagine would be for her to have to continue to suffer in this world, where moth and rust destroy.

This is a promise to us. The children belong to His kingdom. They are the greatest in the kingdom of Heaven. Children! How cherished and welcomed they would be into Heaven.

They are **so loved!** YOU are that treasure. His precious possession. You are a child of God. I didn't have the answers as to why this could possibly happen, but God had answers.

**At the time the disciples came to Jesus, saying, "Who
is the greatest in the kingdom of heaven?" And
calling to him a child, he put him in the midst of them
and said, "Truly, I say to you, unless you turn away
and become like children, you will never enter the
kingdom of heaven. Whoever humbles himself like
this child is the greatest in the kingdom of heaven."
"Beware that you don't look down on any of these
little ones. For I tell you that in heaven their angels
are always in the presence of my Heavenly Father."**
(Matthew 18:1-4 (ESV), 10 (NLT))

God wants to protect these specific children from the pain in this life would inevitably give to them. Their lives and their deaths have become a reflection and a beautifully difficult lesson in how great God's love really is. We don't know why He has given and has taken away, but we do know they are protected and safe, and treasured.

With all the lessons I had learned throughout life, and despite what I had deeply felt, I was wrong. A child's death perhaps wasn't the worst thing that could ever happen. It is the worst thing that could happen to *us*, but not to them. It is perhaps the best thing that could happen to a child- they are forever safe.

The next best thing, is to become like a child again. He wants us all to be like children. To start over; to have new life; to be born again. This time, let your Good Father take care of it all for you. Let Him give you the good gifts; in fact the best gift. The gift of Jesus and the gift of life that doesn't end at death.

He is going to let you learn your lessons, the hard way, but let Him help you navigate through life. He is going to help you to learn how to walk. How to talk. What to eat. Oh my goodness, He even tells us how to dress and to 'clothe ourselves with humility.'

We inevitably want to do it all on our own, like little kids do, and He will give the space and time we need to learn our life lessons, but He never will leave us to do it alone. We do not have this life figured out. We can't do it without our Father.

For our earthly fathers disciplined us for a few years, doing the best they knew how. But God's discipline is always good for us. So we might share in His holiness. No discipline is enjoyable while it is happening- it's painful! But afterward, there will be a peaceful harvest of right living for those who are trained in this way. So take a new grip with your tired hands and strengthen

**your weak knees. Mark out a straight path for your
feet so that those who are weak and lame will not
fall but become strong.**
(Hebrews 12:10-12)

Jesus wasn't going to abandon someone who accepted that love like a child. Even when Jesus was hanging on a cross, the worst moment of his life, a moment even He wanted to get out of if it was God's will, that man could recognize Jesus' compassion, love and power.

Jesus made the same promise he made to children about Heaven to the man who was being crucified beside Him, who maybe didn't have a great father himself. Jesus promised that man who believed that Jesus was who He said He was; I also know children belong with Jesus.

**"Truly, I say to you, today you will
be with me in paradise"**
(Matthew 19:14)

He had the power to defeat death in that moment, and He did what He had to do so he could truly save us from death.

He never abandoned the people who cried out to Him; the ones who recognized the need for Him.

**For God has said, I will never fail you.
I will never abandon you.**
(Hebrews 13:5)

Having that hope and faith was the peace that I needed to fully surrender my life to God's plan; to look past my own grief and to find tangible ways to show love to my God.

My life is completely in His hands. And I could only surrender when I felt like it was all taken away from me, and the only thing left I had was His love for me.

And to understand that when it comes to death, love won. Because love came down, and we were given the choice to choose love. And love brings life.

> **There He will remove the cloud of gloom, the shadow of death than hangs over the earth. He will swallow up death forever! The Sovereign Lord will wipe away all tears. He will remove all insults and mockery against His land and people. The Lord has spoken! In that day, the people will proclaim, "This is our God! We trusted in Him, and He saved us! This is the Lord, in whom we trusted. Let us rejoice in the salvation He brings!"**
> (Isaiah 25:7-9)

It's all I ever need in life. It's all I ever need in death. When everything is stripped away that we treasured here on earth, what remains?

Faith, Hope, and Love! And the greatest, the one that sums it all up in that neat little bow, is Love. The greatest Love. This is our God; our God of love, life and death. King of all!

Now is when we need to turn our lives around and make that choice! There is an hour glass for our lives. We don't physically live forever.

But the one thing you really need to fear in life- don't die a spiritual death. That is the scariest thing. Think about what's at stake. But so many don't want to think about death, so they don't take the time to reflect. Take that time. It's literally a battle between life and death. Choose wisely, my friends.

Wake up! Strengthen what little remains, for even what is left is almost dead. I find your actions do not meet the requirements of my God. Go back to what you heard and believed at first; hold to it firmly. Repent and turn to me again. If you don't wake up, I will come to you suddenly, as unexpected as a thief.

(Revelation 3:2-3)

Sweet Surrender

Be wise in the way you act towards outsiders; make the most of every opportunity. Let your conversation always be gracious, seasoned with salt, so that you may know how to answer everyone.
(Colossians 4:5-6)

Words. While there aren't words to fix a situation like this, I prayed that I would know what to say and do to practically help them through this time.

On the day of the tragedy, between some of the local day home providers, we had discussed that whoever had gone through this tragedy, we wanted, as a community, to support them in whatever way we could.

While it was unknown at the time, it would likely be one of "our children", and we collectively just wanted to support and help, whoever the family was.

That thought of extending support to the family had been immediately imprinted on my mind, even before I knew it was Uta. Whoever it was would be needing support, and lots of it.

Upon discovering that is was Uta and her family, I knew this was on me. It was all I could do. I was so overcome by grief, but I knew I needed to support my friends; this was my priority for the season of life I was about to enter.

But this will be your opportunity to tell the rulers and other unbelievers about Me. When you are arrested, don't worry about how to respond or what to say. God will give you the right words at the right

time. For it is not you who will be speaking- it will be the Spirit of your Father speaking through you.
(Matthew 10:18-20)

I knew beyond all doubt that this was the opportunity God was giving me to point to peace- found only in Jesus. This was the moment I had been literally created for.

I had asked them if I could set up some sort of trust fund or fundraiser to help them financially. The very last thing a parent should worry about it how to arrange a funeral for their baby. With the help of friends, new and old, we set up a fundraiser through a website, hoping to alleviate any financial worries.

Despite feeling incredibly hopeless, I found myself on the radio, trying to rally the support of our community to offer a financial donation to reduce the burden of losing a child.

I could barely speak, yet the words I needed to say came out of my mouth. I also found myself making phone calls to various people, like the funeral director, trying to gather costs of how much money was needed for things like funeral expenses.

Again, the support of the community left me speechless. I was told by the funeral director that they would not be receiving any type of invoice for this funeral. A local church donated the coffin, and the community raised so much money to financially support this family.

Within hours, thousands of dollars had been raised already. There was an outpouring of support from the community. I am so humbled to have been part of this, and so truly astounded by the generosity of people.

The world's best sushi restaurant put on a huge dinner, adding greatly to the financial support the community wanted to offer.

It was a beautiful night where the families and the friends of Uta came together, to cry and to hug and to celebrate the life of a beautiful child who was so loved.

In that restaurant that night, the whole community there in my mind, not only was the best sushi in the world, but also is the best group of people, who became like part of my family.

The reality is there are no words to fix the situation; to take away the pain. It hurts deeply and the grief is unspeakable.

So while there are no words to take back what has happened, there are words of comfort, and support. I found myself writing words I never, ever wanted to write.

Our dear friends, Kaz and Kayo lost their beautiful 15 month old daughter, Uta in a tragic accident. In her short time on this earth, she touched so many lives with love and joy; a legacy that will live on. Our hearts break for this family at the loss of such a precious life- a life that was so full of happiness and love, and gone too soon.

While there are no words or actions we can do to make the situation even remotely bearable, we would like to help them financially, so they have one less stress in this terrible time.

Our amazing community of Revelstoke has been incredibly supportive in this heart breaking situation already, with kind words, prayers, offers of help, and respect. Let's join together as friends and family, and show this incredible family our love.

They have touched so many of our lives in many ways; let's offer them all the support we can.

Financially supporting them is one of the most practical ways we can help them right now. Funds raised will go toward funeral costs, living expenses, time away from their jobs, and future financial plans.

Please let them be able to focus on the value of the funeral process, however they chose to proceed, but not the costs. This is something no parent can ever plan for; any help in this grieving process will be truly appreciated. With love, Friends of Kaz & Kayo.

There were no monetary expectations, but to see the amount given with such generosity is heartwarming. Having a support group that was not limited to our small community for them was incredible. We were and still are so grateful to everyone for supporting and joining together in showing so much love and kindness.

Fundraisers and money will never ease a loss, but the gesture of love means the world. From the bottom of my heart: thank you, thank you, thank you. To witness the love that was shown in those moments in absolute darkness was life changing for so many people.

Thank you so much to each and every person who has shown love and kindness through their words and donations. Words cannot fully express how much comfort this brought. I was beginning to see some light amongst the darkness. It went from having no words, to not having enough words.

Uta's legacy will live on in all of us, and this time will be remembered as the time the world came together to help our friends and show them love in so many ways.

The situation was completely out of my hands, yet God continued to show comfort and His presence to me. I knew, without a doubt that He was so real, and so kind. My eyes were being opened to everything He was doing, and I was able to trust that He was continuing to work this pain out, even in the following years.

When people go through a tragedy together, the opportunities for friendship and love are undeniable. Horrific events really do bring people closer together.

When something as terrible as losing a child happens, very good people and actions do come out from behind the scenes.

There were so many people and businesses who showered this family with love, and it was the first time I had ever seen a community rally their support like that. The outpouring of love was astonishing.

There were no negative words; no judgments; only compassion and love. Sometimes, when tragedies happen, people don't always say the right things. There really aren't words to make it better, but there can certainly are words to make it worse. I encourage you to only use words to build others up; not to tear down.

One thing I feel strongly about though, is to say *something; anything* with kindness and love. You can't go wrong with love.

Saying nothing is only pretending like a painful event never happened; its denial only segregates and isolates a person who is in pain.

It's acknowledging the pain. It's feeling the pain with them. Doing hard time in a personal prison is enough to break a person. You may not understand how they feel if you've never experienced a loss, and you don't need to try to understand. Just cry with them. Send a heart.

Say their child's name. Acknowledge their life. Acknowledge their importance in our lives.

No one knows what to say when a child dies. But supporting them is doing life with them. It's bringing the connection we deeply need with others because that's how we were designed. We aren't meant to be alone. We are meant to do life together.

This is why practical love is important. Bringing food. Making them coffee. Sitting with them in their grief. Taking the burden off their shoulders, just like Jesus did for us.

For the Kingdom of God is not a matter of what we eat or drink, but of living a life of goodness and peace and joy in the Holy Spirit. If you serve Christ with this attitude, you will please God and others will approve of you, too. So then, let us aim for harmony in the church and try to build each other up.

(Romans 14:17-19)

Orange

And just like that, the colour orange began popping up in my life. With my design background, I'll just say, orange is a tricky colour to work with. I was very resistant to the colour orange in décor, even in the fall. It's very in your face. It wants to be seen.

Honestly, it's never been a favourite colour of mine. Yet it kept showing up. It even got to the point where I thought, 'Wow, that is a really bold colour. How am I only noticing it now?'

I was asked by one of my friends organizing Uta's celebration of life if I would speak, if the chance came up. No one wants to speak at a child's funeral, but after more tears, I prepared something to say, just in case.

Thankfully, I didn't end up having to speak. It likely would have been too much for me, but I was prepared for whatever was asked of me. In that moment, I was there to comfort the family without words instead.

Orange was the colour of the cue cards I had chosen for what I had planned to say at Uta's celebration of life. My father in law had just given me a package of multi-coloured fluorescent recipe cards the day of Uta's celebration of life, along with some other comforting items. The thoughtfulness in these small gifts alone was comfort.

Now, recipe cards may be an unlikely present, but as it turned out, I needed them so I could be prepared, should I need to actually speak in front of a crowd. I deliberately thought about what colour I would choose. I was concerned about which colour would be easiest to see with the seemingly never ending tears I was experiencing.

I want to share what I had written down, chosen on those fluorescent orange cue cards.

First of all, I'd like to thank everyone from the bottom of my heart for all the support and generosity and love that has been shown to Kaz and Kayo.

It's beyond words how many lives that Uta's short life has touched. She was so full of joy and life. She was the only one year old who so rarely naps. She knew she didn't have time in her life to waste.

I had the absolute privilege of being able to take care of her over the last couple of months. I feel so lucky to have those moments with Uta given to me. She was so small and in a day home, basically surrounded by wild, fun, action packed two year olds (4 of them!), I pretty much carried her the whole time. Now looking back, what better use of my time than snuggling and kissing a little soul. I am so thankful for that.

Kaz and Kayo are extraordinary parents. They filled Uta's short life with so, so much love. There is something so special about their bond as a family, and that will live on forever.

A few years ago, I was at the Sangha Bean coffee shop, and an older gentleman stopped me, and left me with the words "Love will live". At the time, I thought those words were meant for the tough situation I was in at the moment.

Those words "Love will live" cannot be more true today and every day.

Uta's legacy of love will truly live on, as we've so clearly seen with the outpouring of love and support from this amazing community Kaz and Kayo have chosen as home.

So please, go show love to your family, your friends, your neighbours, the world. And think of Uta and how much love and happiness she has brought to our lives.

Even though I didn't have the opportunity to speak those words in front of anyone, I do feel they are important as part of Uta's legacy is living on through LOVE. They are part of her story; the words that I've been able to reflect on and learn the hardest life lessons.

Just like the colour orange, this idea that love will live kept resurfacing time and time again.

Love will live. Regardless of death, through Jesus, love will live.

Yet, how could God, who loves us, allow this? Could there be reason behind a child's death? I was reminded again and again that His ways are not our ways. While I questioned and wondered why, I turned to God for comfort and understanding.

Families who had lost their children began running through my mind. I thought of Rachel and her family, and of the musician, Steven Curtis Chapman's family, whose experience was so eerily similar to this very situation.

I had remembered that Steven Curtis Chapman's wife, Mary Beth, had written a book on their experience, and I knew I needed to read it as soon as possible. My mother got her hands on a copy, and got it to me.

Kaz had shared with me an idea of a symbol honouring their daughter- an orange flower with eleven petals, with one visibly missing petal.

When my mother handed me the book by Mary Beth Chapman, I burst into tears. One of their daughter's last drawings was there, in the title of her book, "Choosing to See"; an orange centered flower with six petals, coloured in blue, but one petal was not coloured in.

On the backside of her drawing was the word "SEE". This was their tangible answer to their prayer to see God in this unimaginable situation.

There is no way this could be coincidence, only God could coordinate something like this. Those symbols had so much meaning because I could so clearly see the connections.

After reading the book, and gathering incredibly valuable insight from a mother who had gone through the pain of losing a child, I felt like those words, "Choosing to SEE" was exactly what God was doing for me.

In the months that followed, Steven Curtis Chapman, himself, wrote a book called "Between Heaven and the Real World."

To read about the faith of this family after suffering through a loss of their child, I began to see how God can use even the darkest circumstances when we have hope that God has more for us than just this life. We have that promise of life past death.

There is always a plan. God loves us and wants us to trust that. He wants us to know life and love.

In the details, I chose to see. In the helplessness of the situation, we could choose to see how love was working. We can't control what happens. But we can choose to see; we can choose love, we can choose life.

Heaven is the Face
By Steven Curtis Chapman

Heaven is the place where she takes my hand
And leads me to You
And we both run into Your arms
Oh God, I know, it's so much
more than I can dream
It's far beyond anything I can conceive
So God, You know, I'm trusting You until I see
Heaven in the face of my little girl

I truly believe that I will see Uta again, in heaven, and it will be amazing to see her sweet little face again. But when you are struck with death so unexpectedly and personally, the realities of life and our ideas of death are challenged, even defied.

"It's not supposed to be this way", was something that crossed my mind innumerable times. Children aren't meant to die before their parents. It was all so unnatural, and unsettling. It is something that some people truly do not come back from. Without hope, this is an understandable reality.

It's only through surrendering our control to Him. We do not have life under our control. But He does. We can trust that He is good. His plan is good. He is life.

The comfort I received kept coming. My dear friend shared these verses with me in the days after, which I have passed along to people living in grief. Life has shown me more loss since. More brokenness. More separation from love.

> **"All praise to God, the Father of our Lord Jesus Christ.**
> **God is our merciful Father and the source of all comfort.**
> **He comforts us in our troubles so that we can comfort**
> **others. When they are troubled, we will be able to give**
> **them the same comfort God has given us. Our hope**
> **for you is unshaken, for we know that as you share in**
> **our sufferings, you will also share in our comfort."**
> (2 Corinthians 1:3-4, 7)

These were verses that have become part of my anthem of my soul in the years that followed.

Words will never be enough, but one month after Uta's death, I was able to share these words:

The past month has been one of the hardest months of my life. I've experienced such profound pain with my friends in the loss of their daughter, who I had the absolute pleasure of caring for in my day home.

While I will never know [fully] why this happened, I have seen incredible love in our community and in our lives. I remember taking this picture trying to get the lighting right behind her. She looked like an angel to me, I had no idea a week later she would become an angel. She was just starting to speak and she would say "hap, hap" I know she was trying to say happy. And I am so happy she was on this earth for the short time she was.

I've learned more about love, and happiness despite pain, in the past month than I have in my whole life.

I keep going back to a song,
Broken by Lifehouse...

I'm falling apart, I'm barely breathing
With a broken heart that's still beating
In the pain, there is healing
In Your name I find meaning
So I'm holdin' on

Uta, we will see you again. 10.15

Just like I was learning to see beauty in a colour that I had hated, I was learning to see beauty in circumstances I hated, something I pushed away because I didn't like how it felt. I began living in colour and seeing the beautiful things that I had pushed away because I didn't like it.

I still don't entirely understand, and I don't think we will ever be able to answer why this exactly happened, but I do know the lessons I have learned about love and our ideas of death have helped me to take an eternal perspective. Life on earth is finite, but through Jesus, life becomes infinite.

**Yet God has made everything beautiful in its own
time. He has planted eternity in the human heart,
but even so, people cannot see the whole scope of
God's work from beginning to end.**
(Ecclesiastes 3: 11)

Eternity is written in our souls. Inside everyone's deepest
depths of their souls, they hope there is more to life than just
eventually dying and nothing past that.

In my previous experiences with death, I may have again
questioned God as to why He would allow such a tragedy to
strike, especially a family that so clearly loved their daughter.
There was a bigger picture. A picture of perfect love.

God *is* love, and He welcomed that little girl into heaven with
loving tears in His own eyes.

He wept. Not because He was sad for her. She is happy. So
unexplainably happy.

He wept because He knew it hurt us. He was sad with us
because He knew we didn't understand what He was doing.
He was protecting her like the good, good Father He is.

Any parent that loves their children wants to protect them at
all costs, but no parent can completely protect their children
from the future pain and suffering that they will inevitably go
through. This hurts our hearts so deeply, yet I know she will
never have to go through any of this pain.

God knows the unfathomable pain of losing a child; He
understood it before we did. This is not how He ever intended
life to be. He intended life to be full of perfect love and no
death, no brokenness. His perfect plan was a perfect world.

He wants us to go back to our first nature, our very first love. The love of a parent. I thought the pain of losing a child was the worst thing that could happen to us on this earth. Yet, the pain that hurts infinitely deeper is when someone dies who may not have that relationship with Jesus. Yet, when the choice is made to look to Jesus, the greatest joy you can imagine takes place!

I had been writing this book for many years, and it consumed my thoughts daily, but it took me years to connect the dots of the intricacies of the details, both big and small. I felt so stuck, so confused about how to make sense of something like the death of a child. Yet I knew that this was something I needed to try to understand.

The day after Uta's celebration of life, I was invited to attend a women's retreat that I had thought about going to, but something had held me back from signing up.

Honestly now, it probably would have been the last thing I would have wanted to go to, considering the circumstances, but I said yes.

But looking back, that invitation to fill a cancelled spot was God's way of telling me, "You weren't supposed to be there, but you are supposed to be there." God was constantly using the people around me to offer comfort to me, while I was doing my best to offer comfort to my friends, who had just lost their daughter.

Remember how I said my eyes were being opened? I began seeing things that I never saw before. They may seem like little things, or coincidences but every single instance was comfort to me.

It was the literal presence of God comforting me, and it was shown through others comforting me. It was amazing to feel the love and support, and I knew it all came through God. He gave me strength to support my friends through the worst tragedy a parent can go through.

I arrived at the woman's retreat; not knowing what to expect, not knowing if I could hold it together, not wanting to be away from my family, yet not wanting to show my family, particularly my son, how truly sad I was. I was promptly handed a florescent orange schedule, and I then had an understanding of what to expect.

It was going to be bold. It was going to be in my face- the very reason I had disliked the colour. Behind the scenes is where I thought I was meant to be; where I was comfortable.

God took that weekend, and despite my pain and grief, it felt like He literally took my hand, and changed my heart.

When faced with death, suddenly there are things in life that seem a lot more futile than they seemed. That weekend, I was able to forgive myself for all the terrible things I had done to myself and to others in my life; I was able to forgive those who had hurt me, and I began to truly understand love and peace.

I wasn't meant to be there that weekend, but God opened a door of opportunity to lavish love onto my life. God quietly took me in His arms, and I knew it would all be okay. I was loved; so loved. He had this all planned out, just for me. This was the weekend I would come to really understand love.

> **Do not be afraid or discouraged, for the**
> **Lord will personally go ahead of you. He**
> **will neither fail you nor abandon you.**
> (Deuteronomy 31:8)

And He never stopped reminding me that He is there to comfort me, to love me. I came home from that woman's retreat to a beautiful bouquet of flowers, sent anonymously, but all I could see was the beautiful orange Alstroemeria flowers, which was the exact colour of a jacket of Uta's.

Of course, because I was beginning to see all the connections to the colour, I looked up what Alstroemeria flowers represent. (flowermeaning.com)

- **Devotion and mutual support, between two family members or friends**
- **Friendship on a broad scale from acquaintanceship to life-long buds**
- **Withstanding the trials of everyday life**
- **Building your personal life by finding new friends and potential romantic connections**
- **Following your dreams and achieving your aspirations, both in a material and spiritual sense.**

I eventually did find out who sent those flowers to me, and I actually had the pleasure of watching her get baptized on the Sunday, just after the women's retreat. She not only offered her support to me, but we truly gained a friendship that went from acquaintances to "friends forever", as she had recently understood and accepted Jesus's love, which means we will someday be up in heaven together.

We shared comfort with each other, supporting each other through grief and death, because God sends people into our lives to help us. We aren't alone. To have that hope is amazing. When you are able to believe that, it also take the pain from death. The suffering is only temporary.

Heaven and earth will disappear,
but my words will never disappear.
(Matthew 24:35)

Can we be at peace with death? Can we believe that we will be alive past death? Yes, I believe that. I accept it with faith. Life on earth will be gone just like that, but I know in my heart that there is something that lives on forever.

For I know that my Redeemer lives, and at the last he will stand upon the earth. And after my skin has been thus destroyed, yet in my flesh I shall see God.
(Job 19:25-26)

Through my hope in Christ, I can believe that there is something so much more than just this life on earth. I can look at death with a totally different outlook from how death previously made me feel. It is not the end. It is only the beginning of a beautiful journey.

I've gone from feeling hopeless to being so filled with hope because of my faith in Christ. My life does not end at death. I have purpose in life and a future beyond death.

"Good people pass away; the godly often die before their time. But no one seems to care or wonder why. No one seems to understand that God is protecting them from the evil to come. For those who follow godly paths will rest in peace when they die."
(Isaiah 57: 1-2)

When a high school friend of mine died in 2019 along with his family- his wife and two children- while serving orphans in Africa, it was a devastating event, yet their funeral was so incredibly beautiful.

We celebrated together their lives, and the assurance that they were in heaven with Jesus- all of them. There was no doubt in the crowd. I knew I wanted my celebration of life to look like this, when my time comes.

We sang "Raise a Hallelujah" (Bethel Music), and I couldn't help but cry at the line,

> **"Up from the ashes, hope will arise. Death
> is defeated, the King is alive."**

Death's pain is taken away entirely. Defeated. Overcome. Conquered. Dominated. Crushed.

Then, when our dying bodies have been transformed into bodies that will never die, this scripture will be fulfilled:

> *Death is swallowed up in victory.*
> *O death, where is your victory?*
> *O death, where is your sting?*

> **For sin is the sting that results in death, and the law gives sin its power. But thank God! He gives us victory over sin and death through our Lord Jesus Christ. So my dear brothers and sisters, be strong and immovable. Always work enthusiastically for the Lord, for you know that nothing you do for the Lord is ever useless.**
> (1 Corinthians 15: 54-58)

This was all predicted and anticipated over the years. The only problem was that people had an expectation that Jesus was going to be a victorious king to conquer Rome. Can you imagine if we limited God to our own expectation?

His plans are far, far greater, even if they feel disappointing in the moment. Jesus literally fulfilled everything in the Bible that had been written hundreds of years before He actually arrived on earth, from the first battle between good and evil to the last battle. And we know who the winner is.

He came as a perfect, little, helpless baby who was so treasured by God. Not what the world was expecting. Yet the road map of death's defeat was at the cost of Jesus's life. The ultimate sacrifice of a perfect life for many broken lives.

He was despised and rejected- a man of sorrows, acquainted with deepest grief. We turned our backs on Him and looked the other way. He was despised, and we did not care. Yet it was our weakness he carried; it was our sorrows that weighed Him down. And we thought His troubles were a punishment from God, a punishment for His own sins! But He was pierced for our rebellion, crushed for our sins. He was beaten so we could be whole. He was whipped so we could be healed. All of us, like sheep, have strayed away. We have left God's paths to follow our own. Yet the Lord laid on Him the sins of us all.
(Isaiah 53: 3-6)

Lost and Found

Jesus knew the pain of losing a friend's life; the shortest verse in the Bible addresses it.

John 11:35 simply says,
"Jesus wept."

He knew He would overcome death, but he still felt the grief we deeply feel. He still cried with his friends and shared the sorrow that comes with death. He took the time to humbly shed tears and to feel the sadness. He didn't walk into the situation with arrogance and ability. He went in and cried with those who were suffering.

He comforted His grieving friends and wept not for the death of his friend, but because He was human. Death hurts. He cried because He shared the grief of death, or separation. He cried to show His friends here, with Him on earth, that He knows. He knows your pain. Your brokenness.

The comfort of suffering with others brings an unexpected connection; a deep friendship like no other. It cannot be explained, and it's something that is unfathomable to others when you experience that level of connection.

Now may our Lord Jesus Christ himself and God our Father, who loved us and by His grace gave us eternal comfort and a wonderful hope, comfort you and strengthen you in every good thing you do and say.
(2 Thessalonians 2:16)

He knew pain, He knew our grief, He could absolutely relate to us. He also knew the big picture. He wept and then raised

His friend from the dead so we could see that He has control over even death.

And just as He raised His friend from the dead, He went to the cross and died Himself so we could become friends. He made a willing choice to follow the big plan; to die a humiliating, excruciating death. Jesus went to the grave to fight for your life so we could become friends- literal friends of God. He wants us to have the joy of friendship in our lives.

I have told you these things so you will be filled with my joy. Yes, your joy will overflow! This is my commandment: Love each other the same way I loved you. There is no greater love than to lay down one's life for one's friends. You are my friends if you do what I command. I no longer call you slaves, because a master doesn't confide in his slaves. Now you are my friends, since I have told you everything the Father told me. You didn't choose me. I chose you. I appointed you to go and produce lasting fruit, so that the Father will give you whatever you ask for, using my name. This is my command: Love each other.
(John 15:11-17)

There is no greater love than this. How much deeper is the love of a Father who lost His only Son *for you.* He knows that pain. That was what it cost Him to prove your worth; your value.

Earth's perfection was shattered by our choices in this life; by our human nature, the reality of growing up and deciding we don't need our parents anymore; we've got this. Then it all falls apart because we thought we knew better.

As we lose our childhood, we all begin to experience the reality of pain and suffering through life. The moment in life comes that we feel the need to control our own lives, yet in that moment was when I realized how lost I was.

> **"For the Son of Man came to save the lost. What do you think? If a man has a hundred sheep, and one of them has gone astray, does he not leave the ninety-nine on the mountains and go in search of the one that went astray? And if he finds it, truly, I say to you, he rejoices over it more than over the ninety-nine that never went astray. So it is not the will of my Father who is in heaven that one of these little ones should perish."**
> (Matthew 18:11-14)

He throws a party when this happens. He doesn't want just a friendship with us while we are here on earth. He wants us to come home, to His house. His amazing house- heaven. This is the thing he wants most of all, and for all of us. This is why we were created.

> **"But his father said to the servants, "Quick! Bring the finest robe in the house and put it on him. Get a ring for his finger and sandals for his feet. And fill the calf we have been fattening. We must celebrate with a feast, for this son of mine was dead and has now returned to life. He was lost but now he is found. So the party began."**
> (Luke 15:22-24)

He literally throws us a party because we came back to Him, where we can now rest and be taken care of by our Father. He can take away every tear, every pain away from us, and let us enjoy the absolute freedom of being a child again. That is the closest we ever are to having a perfect, carefree life.

The question has come up in life- if there is, in fact, a heaven, what will we look like when we die and go to heaven?

But someone may ask, "How will the dead be raised?
What kind of bodies will they have?" What a foolish
question! When you put a seed into the ground, it
doesn't grow into a plant unless it dies first.
And what you put into the ground is not the plant that
will grow, but only a bare seed of wheat or whatever you
are planting. Then God gives it the new body He wants it
to have. A different plant grows from each kind of seed.
...It is the same way with the resurrection of the dead.
Our earthly bodies are planted in the ground when we
die, but they will be raised to live forever. Our bodies are
buried in brokenness, but they will be raised in glory.
They are buried in weakness, but they will be raised in
strength. They are buried as natural human bodies, but
they will be raised as spiritual bodies. For just as there
are natural bodies, there are also spiritual bodies.
(1 Corinthians 15:35-38; 42-44)

I think we become children again when we die. It all makes
sense. He talks about children being the greatest in heaven. He
talks about us being His special possessions and about storing
treasures in heaven. He often refers to those in heaven being
His children.

And they will never die again. In this respect
they will be like angels. They are children of
God and children of the resurrection.
(Luke 21:36)

He wants us to become like children again; His children,
and he only wants you to admit that you need the Father. I'm
sorry Dad, I didn't know better than you. Take me back. He
wants to give us our lives back, and the very best days of our
lives. The days we were unburdened by pain, cared for, and
unconditionally loved.

The Underdog

Throughout the years, as I've been working on this book, I've often felt discouraged and haven't always known what to say. I have felt like I don't understand enough of the Bible to say anything about it, but what I do know is that my life- the good and the bad- has been molded into a part of who I am today.

I'm still not perfect, and I never will be, but I know God can use me, and that God can take the brokenness of me and my life. And He loves me anyways. He can and He has changed my life into something that I could have never imagined.

This book has helped me make sense of so much in this life, and I believe God uses the most unlikely people to do His work. I didn't even have the confidence to tell very many people I was working on this.

But nothing I do for Jesus is useless, even the things I've felt were mistakes; and even the things that *were* most definitely mistakes. The biggest lessons I needed to learn, had to be learned deeply and honestly. It's not because He wants us to suffer. He wants us to truly understand.

It's so He can lead us into peace, and into joy, and into true love. That is real life; a life where you are so loved, forever.

I pray that God, the source of hope, will fill you completely with joy and peace because you trust in Him. Then you will overflow with confident hope through the power of the Holy Spirit.
(Romans 15:13)

I have that confidence now. I know, with all my heart that this life I've got, and everything that I am, is in His hands, not mine. He's got this. I don't. And I am so thankful for that.

He provided me with the strength to keep going when I couldn't get out of bed. He gave me the stubbornness to never quit during the darkest times. He gave me the desire to seek understanding. He gave me the opportunities to mess up, and to still love me, and never give up on me. He gave me the heart I have because He knew I wouldn't give up either.

> **Love is patient and kind, love does not envy or boast; it is not arrogant or rude. It does not insist on its own way; it is not irritable or resentful; it does not rejoice at wrongdoing, but rejoices with truth. Love bears all things, believes all things, hopes all things, endures all things. Love never ends. So now faith, hope and love abide, these three; but the greatest of these is love.**
> (1 Corinthians 13: 4-8, 13)

The description of love sounds like the effects God was doing in my life. God *is* love. God can use my stories to bring amazement and wonder to Him. I couldn't make up the things that happened, and because I can't even process how absolutely amazing He is. I'm blown away on a daily basis.

He is in every step of the process. He is in every detail, and He will continue to work in lives of those whom He chooses. I have that hope, and God has the ability to make it happen.

God is so patient. Those lessons have taken so much time to sink in. But God has carved out time for me to finish this story; to press on towards the goal. Time has not run out for me. Perhaps, this is only the beginning.

I don't mean to say that I have already achieved these things or that I have already reached perfection. But I press on to possess that perfection for which Christ Jesus first possessed me. No, dear brothers and sisters, I have not achieved it, but I focus on this one thing: Forgetting the past and looking forward to what lies ahead, I press on to reach the end of the race and receive the heavenly prize for which God, through Christ Jesus, is calling us.
(Philippians 3:12-14)

My hope is that I leave behind a legacy of love, like Uta's short life has done; and like the many funerals I have attended of those who love Jesus. I want them to say, she was pretty broken, but she loved because He loved her. She loved as best she could, and kept trying to reflect that in her life. I want a legacy that only points to Jesus and His love.

We love because He first loved us.
(1 John 4:10)

We likely will never know the effects we fully have on another person. "You don't know what you've got 'til it's gone" is a very true saying. Sometimes, we only realize what we had after they are gone. Don't let love go unsaid to others. Don't let go of the chance to love when you have it.

My entire purpose is to reflect the love of Jesus to our world. Even though I was so broken and flawed, everything about my life has been a lesson in love; true love. That love will bring peace and joy.

I don't know why He chose me, but maybe He knew it would be an alright story to use in the end. It is only because of God's *amazing grace* that He chooses the people He does.

**For I am the least of all the apostles*. In fact, I'm not
even worthy to be called an apostle after the way I
persecuted God's church. But whatever I am not, it
is all because God poured out His special favour on
me- and not without results. For I have worked harder
than any of the other apostles; yet it was not I, but
God who was working through me by His grace.**
(1 Corinthians 15: 9-10)

"Apostle" definition: Greek- "one who is sent off";

In modern English: Friends and followers of Jesus. Please like
and subscribe for more content.

Throughout the Bible, he uses some real losers. Think David
and Goliath. Unlikely superheroes. The underdog. It's almost
embarrassing sometimes.

I always think when people accuse the Bible of being full of
lies, and I go, *'If it was a book of lies, I personally would make my
main characters out to be way more awesome.'*

**Instead, God chose things the world considers
foolish in order to shame those who think they are
wise. And he chose things that are powerless to
shame those who are powerful.**
(1 Corinthians 1:27)

I've sometimes thought to myself, you can't make this stuff up.
It's unbelievable. It doesn't make sense. That's why I wrote as
much as I did. I didn't want the details to be missed, because
I do want to understand the bigger picture.

These people, just like me, had no idea what their lives were
purposed for. They had no idea what to say or what to do.

**Don't worry about how to defend yourself or what to say,
for the Holy Spirit will teach you what needs to be said.**
(Luke 12:11-12)

That's okay! God's got this. You just need to ask, seek, and knock. He will open those doors and you just need to follow Him.

I don't know why He chose me to write this story, I don't know why He took Uta and Rachel and all the other children off this earth. We thought it was too soon to lose these people, but I know that they have perfect peace.

Their lives have taught me so much. I began cherishing every moment I had, especially with my own family. But more than that, I realized my greatest purpose in life is not just to enjoy life with those who I love, but to point everyone who has come across my path to Jesus.

He was taking every moment in my life and making it intentional. If it was up to me, I'd still be connecting the dots. He lined everything up perfectly, and because I had learned to praise Him in the storms, He helped me figure things out.

Even if I failed, God still had it under control. He wants us to have an easy life. He just wants to save us from ourselves; we are our own worst enemies.

**But for those who are righteous, the way is not steep
and rough. You are a God who does what is right, and
You smooth out the path ahead of them. Lord, we show
our trust in You by obeying your laws; our hearts
desire it to glorify Your name.**
(Isaiah 26:7-8)

God knows life is going to be a rough path for us if we don't trust Him. Not if we aren't righteous or perfect. Which is impossible, humanly speaking. We can't do it alone.

As the scriptures say, "No one is righteous- not even one. No one is truly wise; no one is seeking God. All have turned away; all have become useless. No one does good, not a single one."
(Romans 3:10-12)

It's Time

**He will keep you strong so that you will be free
from all blame on the day when our Lord Jesus
returns. God will do this, for He is faithful to
do what He says, and He has invited you into
partnership with His Son, Jesus Christ our Lord.**
(1 Corinthians 1:8-9)

Just as I heard the words, "Love will live" in a coffee shop,
which were words that truly changed the course of my life in
searching for the meaning behind those mysterious words,
my pastor saw these words on two separate people's T-shirts.

"Time is not over"

"Forever is too late"

Not to be overly dramatic, but it's going to happen someday.
Your life on earth has an expiry date, whether you are a child
or you made it to 100. You don't know exactly when, but it'll be
sooner than you think. Turn back to Him. He will show you
the easier path to life.

**The end of the world is coming soon. Therefore, be
earnest and disciplined in your prayers. Most important
of all, continue to show deep love for each other, for
love covers a multitude of sins.**
(1 Peter 4:7-8)

Don't wait until it's too late. Death rarely comes with much
notice. It's a thief. Time is a thief. Death is a thief. That is the
ultimate deception of death. Death's only grand finale is if love
is rejected. It does not have to be that way. Just choose today!

Again and again that flood will come,
morning after morning, day and night
until you are carried away."
This message will bring terror to your people.
(Isaiah 28:19)

So quit procrastinating, delaying or blatantly refusing. Look up and store your treasure- your life and your love, in heaven where it will be safe. This life isn't over with the finality of death that we fear, if we have the hope that life has no end.

Love never ends. Time ends.

"Behold, the days are coming," declares the Lord God,
"when I will send a famine on the land- not a famine
of bread, nor a thirst for water, but of hearing the
words of the Lord. They shall wander from sea to sea,
from north to south, they shall run to and fro, to seek
the word of the Lord, and they shall not find it."
(Amos 8:11-12)

People are searching for love. They really are. They will look for it anywhere. In rocks, in organized religion, in others, in work. They will look everywhere, except up. Look up! Look to nature- can't you see there HAS to be a creator? This all just happened? From the biggest to the smallest details. Open your eyes!

"Who does the Lord think we are?" they ask.
"Why does He speak to us like this? Are we
little children just recently weaned?
He tells us everything over and over- one line at a time,
one line at a time, a little here and a little there."
(Isaiah 28:9-10)

Despite the stubbornness of my heart in learning about love, despite my absolute brokenness, despite the amount of time it took for me to realize the lessons He had been trying to teach me all along, He did it with patience and tenderness of a very, very, very loving Father.

I had to learn the lessons over and over and over. We need it repeated over and over before we finally see the truth!

God has told His people, "Here is a place of rest; let the weary rest here. This is a place of quiet rest. But they would not listen. So the Lord will spell out His message for them again, one line at a time, one line at a time, a little here, a little there, so that they will stumble and fall. They will be injured, trapped and captured.
(Isaiah 28:12-13)

He wants us to be set apart and different from everything this world is trying to tell us to be. Holy means to be set apart. He wants us to be so set apart, he repeats it over and over and over. Holy, holy, holy.

God is trying to show us the best way to live our lives; how to live in peace. So we can rest. Rest in Peace. He knows the whole plan for each one of us, but most will never listen; either because they don't understand or they just don't care.

You are His treasure. This is the type of belonging we all long for. It's a friendship that will never let us down; a relationship fulfilling every desire we didn't even know we longed for. He is the connection that will piece our shattered lives together, making beauty from the ashes.

"For you were made from dust, and to dust you will return."
(Genesis 3:19)

There is so much beauty in life, and we can trust that death is not the whole picture in life. It's not over at the death of our bodies- it's only over if we die and we are spiritually dead. That is something to fear.

He can take your broken life and fix it. It can be an incredibly painful process, but it is so much easier of a path when you know you are so loved, no matter what you have done.

Trust in the Lord with all your heart, do not lean on your own understanding. In all your ways, acknowledge Him, and He will make straight your paths.
(Proverbs 3:5-6)

Just trust Him. Believe that He loves you so much that He sent His Son to die on a cross for you and me, then raised Him from the dead, so that if you could believe that, you'd know that God has control over life and death.

Don't be afraid of those who want to kill your body; they cannot touch your soul. Fear only God, who can destroy both soul and body in hell.
(Matthew 10:28)

Trust that death is defeated when His love for us is accepted, by us. He did this so you could see, with your eyes wide open, that if He could control death with love, you can trust that He will fulfill a promise of life with Him forever. We have nothing to fear if we know God can control death.

Everything that Jesus speaks is love. Because He is the perfect promised sacrifice. There is so much love in those red letters of your dusty Bible. There is love that you can see in the orange; in the rainbow of colours! Don't live in the shadow, in the ashes anymore. What beauty from the ashes! What hope we have in the colours!

God loves making broken things beautiful; mended together with the most precious thing on earth- mended Wabi-Sabi style, with gold as the glue, because you are a treasure. A beautifully broken treasure. He wants to restore you because you are so valuable to Him.

It's hard to understand, so ask for understanding. Ask. Seek answers. Trust that when you knock, only He can make your life into what it is meant to be. God will send people running into your life to help you to understand the depths of this truth.

He has a good plan for you, and your life. He wants goodness for you. He's also got a plan for your death, and that's a choice in your hands. Choose today! Do it before it's too late for you.

Following Him on your path of life is the simplest thing, yet the hardest. It's not easy to trust. It doesn't make sense in our minds. It's complicated, complex, beyond our knowledge. But He is our perfect example. We don't know the beginning from end. But He has the whole picture.

Yet, not trusting? I can, with 100% confidence tell you, that's not an easy path. The alternative to not trusting His plan will only lead to pain and death. But trusting in the purest, kindest, most true love? This is the narrow path, but it is a good path.

You only need to get to the point in your path, straight or narrow, to knock on that door, then walk through it and follow Him. He will help you with the rest.

In that day He will be your sure foundation, providing a rich store of salvation, wisdom and knowledge. The fear of the Lord will be your treasure.
(Isaiah 33:6)

He will make you whole again. You're missing something in your life and it's Jesus! He will rebuild your life. He will fix your foundations. And even if it burns down, don't worry! That house isn't the house for you. (Disclaimer: not literally, this is figuratively!!)

For no one can lay any foundations other than the one we already have- Jesus Christ!
(1 Corinthians 3:11)

I add the disclaimer because, I kid you not, we had looked at a house when I was pregnant that we thought was good enough. We were getting desperate. I prayed, asking for a sign to know if this house was 'the one', and that house BURNED TO THE GROUND.

Your house on earth isn't good enough. He's got a kingdom waiting for you, and He can't wait to throw a party to welcome you home. You are the homecoming king and queen, heirs to the Throne of God!

Some of you will rebuild the deserted ruins of your cities. Then you will be known as a rebuilder of walls and a restorer of homes.
(Isaiah 58:12)

Let him rebuild your house; let Him fix those crumbling, shattered foundations. You can't do it. It is impossible, but so was bringing people back to life. He brings life after death, literally and figuratively. No disclaimer needed.

Stand firm against him [the devil], and be strong in your faith. Remember that your family of believers all over the world is going through the same kind of suffering you are. In His kindness God called you to share in His eternal glory by means of Christ Jesus. So

after you have suffered a little while, he will restore, support and strengthen you, and He will place you on a firm foundation. All power to Him forever! Amen.
(1 Peter 5:9-11)

Stop. Turn around. Run back to Him! And if your house is literally burning, you know that you need to 'Stop, Drop and Roll!'

Save your life! He is trying to save you from the fire of death and hell. Recognize that. Accept that love from your Father. Acknowledge His love, stop ignoring it. Open your eyes!

There are lots of keys and lots of doors out there, but there is only one key to life's door. He is the only way.

"Don't be afraid! I am the First and the Last. I am the living one. I died, but look- I am alive forever and ever! And I hold the keys of death and the grave."
(Revelation 1:18)

So say His name! Acknowledge Him- our Good Father. Call out to Jesus, call to the Father to save your life. He has already won the battle against death.

His bottomless, regardless love was shown to us by that. He will take you on a beautiful journey. It won't always be easy, but it will be better. Just trust Him. He's got this.

Don't forget who created the universe. Our creator! Say His name so the people around you know He is not forgotten. He knows what you were created for. He is your creator! He is the only plan. Plan A, not plan B. Life or death. Choose today!

Then thank Him. And do your best, not because you are perfect, but because you are so loved. And love Him right back.

I haven't always been faithful in everything, but He draws me back to Him time and time again. So I don't give up, and I continue to draw my life near to Him.

There is nothing more I want than to stand before Him in His love and hear Him say,

'Well done, my good and faithful servant. You have been so faithful in handling this small amount, so I will give you many more responsibilities. Let's celebrate together!
(Matthew 25:21)

Time isn't over for me. And when my time is over, and I will stand in front of my God, my Saviour, my King. I'll look at Him and say, "I did it because I love you. But I did it because You loved me first. It's all You. I am nothing without You! It all started with You, and it will all end with You. My God who gives never- ending love and life."

The beginning and the end. The first and the last.
The Way. The Truth. The Life.

All we can do is our best with the knowledge we have. At the end of this life on earth, after leaving my house, my life, my legacy, as much as I know about who God is, I want to meet God in His kingdom. No more pain, no more tears.

All we have to do is ask and receive and accept His love. His perfect peace. His perfect joy. His perfect love. Forever we are loved. And forever we can rest in His perfect, love. We can rest in peace. This is the way to true life.

Three things will last forever- faith, hope and love- and the greatest of these is love.
(1 Corinthians 13: 13)

Love will live.

Jesus told him, "I am the Way, the Truth, and the Life. No one can come to the Father, except through me. If you had really known Me, you would know who my Father is. From now on you do know Him and have seen Him!"

Jesus replied, "All who love me will do what I say. My Father will love them, and we will come and make our home with each of them. Anyone who doesn't love me will not obey me. And remember, my words are not my own. What I am telling you is from the Father who sent me. I am telling you these things now while I am still with you. But when the Father sends the Advocate as my representative—that is, the Holy Spirit—he will teach you everything and will remind you of everything I have told you. "I am leaving you with a gift—peace of mind and heart. And the peace I give is a gift the world cannot give. So don't be troubled or afraid.

Remember what I told you: I am going away, but I will come back to you again. If you really loved me, you would be happy that I am going to the Father, who is greater than I am. I have told you these things before they happen so that when they do happen, you will believe. "I don't have much more time to talk to you, because the ruler of this world approaches. He has no power over me, but I will do what the Father requires of me, so that the world will know that I love the Father. Come, let's be going."
(John 14:6-7; 23-30)

Printed in the United States
by Baker & Taylor Publisher Services